BEHOLD, I SHINE

Freny Manecksha is an independent journalist, published in *Himāl Southasian* and *The Times of India: Crest Edition*, among other publications, who has reported extensively from Kashmir, covering human rights and development issues. She has also worked with *The Times of India* and *The Indian Express*. Freny lives in Mumbai.

BEHOLD, I SHINE

NARRATIVES OF KASHMIR'S WOMEN AND CHILDREN

Freny Manecksha

RUPA

Published by
Rupa Publications India Pvt. Ltd 2017
7/16, Ansari Road, Daryaganj
New Delhi 110002

Sales centres:
Allahabad Bengaluru Chennai
Hyderabad Jaipur Kathmandu
Kolkata Mumbai

ISBN: 978-81-291-4571-0

First impression 2017

10 9 8 7 6 5 4 3 2 1

The moral right of the author has been asserted.

To free spirits and champions of azadi everywhere

Contents

PREFACE ix

INTRODUCTION xix
A Brief History of Kashmir

A SOLDIER UNDER A CHINAR 1
Navigating Kashmir's Morphed Landscape

JOSH THA, JAWAN THAY 15
Women's Call for Azadi in the 1990s

WHO KILLED MY SON 28
The Wounded Spectators of the 1990s

DON'T THINK, MY CHILD 42
The Tehreek Generation

HOW DO I TELL MY STORY? 56
Sexual Violence in the Valley

MAINE NAZIRA, AA KHA? 78
Memory as Women's Resistance

UMEED HAI 95
Women Seeking Justice in Kashmir

WHERE ELSE CAN I GO?   108
Women, Spirituality and the Valley

CONCERN OR CONTROL?   115
The Complexities of Occupation

I CAN SAVE MYSELF   125
Dissent and Feminism in a New Millenium

EPILOGUE   139

ACKNOWLEDGEMENTS   145

PREFACE

In 2010, my interest in the troubled state of Kashmir was sparked by a list—'Body Count'—that began appearing on my Facebook newsfeed. It was a tabulated catalogue, created by journalist Dilnaz Boga, of all the unarmed civilians killed in the violence of that year in Kashmir—beginning with the death of sixteen-year-old Inayat Khan on 8 January 2010.

The ever-increasing toll of fatalities—largely of youth—made me very uneasy. Were these young boys and even some girls actually being paid by Pakistan—as the Indian government claimed—to throng the streets, throw stones and get killed? Media reports were fragmented and inchoate—they could not present a comprehensive picture. In October 2010, impelled by curiosity, I accepted Dilnaz's invitation to come to Srinagar and gather first-hand impressions.

During my week-long stay in the Valley, I travelled with her and other reporters. I heard of local ambulances being stopped and relatives getting beaten up by security forces and of assaults in internationally accepted 'safe' places like hospitals. These accounts brought about a quantum shift in my perceptions of the region. It also marked the beginning of the Kashmir chapter of my life. I felt an overwhelming need to revisit it, not as a tourist, but as someone who wished to understand the 'terrible beauty' of this land and its people.

(It was with a dreadful sense of déjà vu that I read of the horrors of 2010 being perpetrated with greater intensity in 2016.)

When I returned to Kashmir, seven months later, in 2011, I learnt of another name on 'Body Count'—Haneefa Begum Wani of Kreeri, Baramulla. I was told that she had been shot and paralyzed the previous summer, when she had stepped out of her home during a spell of consecutive curfews spanning thirty-five days. After months of struggling to survive, Haneefa finally succumbed to her injuries.

I wondered what compelled Haneefa to defy curfew orders? Was she, as some media reports suggested, one among the hundreds of angry protesters who had rushed to the streets after the student, Farrukh Bukhari went 'missing' and was later found dead?

Looking for answers, I visited Haneefa's home in May 2011, along with Kashmiri journalist Izhar Ali. Haneefa, a divorcee, used to live in these quarters with her parents, brothers and her young daughter Humaira.[1] The family offered a narrative at variance with media reports. They insisted that Haneefa's 'crime' was that she was a mother desperately seeking medical attention when her child was down with typhoid fever.

Haneefa's brother Abdullah Wani told me, 'My sister left home on 31 July 2010, saying that she would take her daughter

---

[1]Haneefa's story has been reported by the author in 'A Death in the Family', *India Together*, in <http://indiatogether.org/shot-human-rights>, 20 July 2011, accessed on 22 July 2016. Humaira's (and by extension Haneefa's) story has been documented by Abid Rashid Baba, 'Orphans of Conflict', *Alternative Kashmir*, in <http://www.alternatekashmir.com/index.php/orphans-of-conflict-2/>, 28 November 2013, accessed on 22 July 2016. Haneefa's name has been spelt as Hanifa in some reports.

to the block hospital, barely a kilometre away. There had been no protests that day and a group of Central Reserve Police Force (CRPF) personnel on the streets had told her that it was okay to proceed. A little later, two more CRPF personnel suddenly appeared, waving their guns. Haneefa spotted them, got alarmed, and began fleeing the scene with her child—but they shot at her retreating figure. She received five bullets on her back. The CRPF men tried to drag her still body, face down, across the street, when people, who had heard the gunshots, came rushing out of their homes. But it was too late—Haneefa had already suffered terrible injuries.'

A medical report shown to me stated that the seventh dorsal vertebra bore the brunt of the bullets and this had led to her paralysis. Haneefa was taken to the block hospital and then had to be shifted to the Sher-i-Kashmir Institute of Medical Sciences (SKIMS). Abdullah said that the ambulance in which they accompanied Haneefa was stopped at least twice during the journey to Srinagar and the family severely beaten up.

Haneefa's distraught mother Raja Begum added, 'I used to worry about my elder daughter who suffers from diabetes. But never in my wildest dreams did it occur to me that something would happen to Haneefa. What do we do now?'

Haneefa's brother said, 'We will take care of Humaira, but how do we make up for a mother's love?'

I will never know decisively who the real Haneefa was or why she was on the streets. Was she indeed a protester—someone whose fierce sense of justice made her decry a young boy's killing—or was she a mother whose love for her daughter made her break curfew orders and seek medical help?

What I do know is that Haneefa was a single woman—who left her husband when he took a second wife and vowed to remain her daughter's sole provider. She took on this responsibility despite the difficulties. This woman had been shot.

The abiding image I carry of that visit is of eleven-year-old Humaira—her head bowed, sitting in the garden. Her face seemed frozen as she gazed at the white tufts of poplar blossoms swirling in the breeze. She had borne witness to her mother being gunned down, suffering and then dying, and was now being provided for by Haneefa's ageing parents and brothers. Abdullah told me that Humaira was a quiet child and rarely interacted with other children.

In 2015, when I inquired after Humaira's whereabouts, I was told that she remained at her nanihal (grandmother's home). She was doing well in school and wished to become a doctor and fulfil her mother's dreams.

The day I visited Humaira's home marked the beginning of a new journey for me—of studying the impact of militarization in the Valley and on the lives of women and children, the most vulnerable sections of society.

◆

It is often assumed that the women of Kashmir have not suffered the brunt of direct violence as much as the men there have done. But is this really true? Or is the scale of their suffering underestimated because it is difficult to access women's stories? Also, what of the indirect violence that has been inflicted on them—shouldn't that be accounted for?

Haneefa Begum Wani's death and the cruel plight of many single women, widows and half-widows,[2] among others,

---

[2]The term half-widow was coined in Kashmir in the nineties for a woman whose husband suffered enforced disappearance and remains untraceable.

sparked within me an urge to calibrate this gender-sensitive lens to consider how Kashmiri families and communities had been ruptured by militarization and examine how women, and children especially, had been impacted.

Many such complex questions arose as I began to view incidents through this perspective. For instance: What really happens to a woman whose husband has 'disappeared'? She is left in a state of emotional limbo, yes, but she also has to confront the daunting task of coping with huge economic loss. Besides, there are challenges that both she and her children must contend with while negotiating domestic spaces. Can a woman whose husband has disappeared stay with her in-laws? Or must she be forced to go back to her childhood home? What will be her status in such a household? Will she be 'allowed' to take decisions regarding her own future and that of her children? Will she be allowed to remarry? Or is this decision the prerogative of her in-laws?

Does militarization harden patriarchal structures? What are the restrictions, or the forces of control and domination, that impact the choices that Kashmiri women can make?

Are their daily negotiations relatively simpler? For instance, can a girl-child attend early morning tuition classes even if it means having to pass by troops standing on the road or a bunker? Or are they complex? For instance, should a half-widow risk visiting an army checkpost to get information about her missing husband?

How do notions of security interact with the patriarchal belief that the rights of a girl-child are less consequential

---

Several enforced disappearances took place in Kashmir when troops would round up men and herd them away to interrogation centres. Many never returned.

than those of a boy? For example, is it concern for a college girl's safety, or, in fact, the thinking that her education is of no consequence that guides decisions whether she is to be 'allowed' to travel to another town to continue her education? Does 'concern' for a woman actually connote 'control' over her?

Has the conflict in Kashmir impacted the degree to which men—and more so, women—can freely access open spaces? How have the traditional recreational areas that were once dominated by children or women—parks and gardens, *yaarbals* or washing ghats, *badamwaris* or almond gardens—been eroded, making even a leisurely stroll a luxury? Or have they transformed—just as areas that were once playgrounds for children are now serving as graveyards? Or is access coloured by circumstance—so, streets that may traditionally be viewed as unsafe—become arenas for mobilization during protests and funerals with women forcefully asserting themselves in the crowds?

If public spaces are dying or transforming, and if the mobility of women and children is curtailed, especially during periods of curfew and unrest, how does this affect the people's emotional health? How do young girls cope with the overwhelming number of restrictions in the Valley? Is the young Kashmiri working woman, who spoke to me, the exception rather than the rule, when she said, 'It just gets so suffocating. All I want to do is spend time outside with my friends and just talk, and talk, and talk?'

Equally, has militarization led to restrictions on clothing and behaviour, or is it the militants who are imposing such 'rules'? Or is it the case that many Kashmiri women have chosen certain dress codes as a means of asserting a new Muslim identity and as a statement of resistance?

Then, there are disquieting and complex questions about sexual violence. A male-dominated society views those women who have been assaulted as having brought 'dishonour' to the village or the family. The women of Kunan-Poshpora—the twin hamlets that witnessed mass rapes in 1991[3]—felt stigmatized for years. A beautiful young girl who had been brutally assaulted by a high-ranking police official in Kupwara confided that she was now perceived as 'spoiled goods'. People in her village taunted her with sexual innuendoes or came up to her father with indecent proposals. Violence, consequently, was being perpetrated at two levels—both by the state's institutions and also by some sections of society within.

What are these women's own understanding of sexual violence? Do they feel that they are to be blamed and that they have done a disservice to their family or community? Conversely, is there a growing inclination to see assault as a political act—to view sexual violence as an integral weapon of war? Does such political awareness encourage women to come forward, name their perpetrators and demand justice?

What about domestic violence? Do patriarchal structures brush aside domestic violence? Are Kashmiri women thinking of gender rights beyond the ambit of the casualties that come with conflict?

And then—a question that demands answers—what about the *tehreek-e-azadi* or freedom movement? Some of the most passionate proponents of azadi and willing participants in

---

[3]'On the night of 23 February 1991, personnel of the 4 Rajputana Rifles of the Indian Army cordoned off the two villages Kunan and Poshpora in north Kashmir's Kupwara district during an anti-insurgency operation and allegedly gangraped at least twenty-three women—with some estimates placing it at around forty.' See Abhishek Saha, 'Kunan-Poshpora: A Forgotten Mass-rape Case of 2 Kashmir Villages,' *Hindustan Times*, 8 February 2016.

the *tehreek* have been women. But as young Farhana Latief, a legal professional and research student, feels compelled to ask, 'Have we really been granted space for crucial decision-making or assertiveness?'

How, then, does one assess the Kashmiri woman's role in the time of conflict? Are her sacrifices to be acknowledged only within the domestic sphere? Are her attempts at facilitating and providing a crucial support to the freedom movement been underplayed? Is this all a part of a narrative of 'gender-forgetting'?

◆

With these pressing questions in mind, I began trying to ferret out women's voices. This meant having to relearn the rules that guide journalism. As journalists, we are trained to use the basics of 'when, where and how' to start work on our stories, demand the exact chronology of events complete with the dates and place a huge emphasis on First Information Reports (FIRs). But all these guidelines need to become flexible in a land where conflict has rendered all things very complex and layered.

Is it fair to assume that an event—overlooked by newspapers—has not happened? Does a rape cease to be a rape if the woman in question is the wife of a militant and, therefore, deemed as a suspect by the state?

On the flip side, how reliable is memory? Can prolonged trauma make remembrance selective or prone to error? Equally, is it possible that some knowledge simply won't be shared—even if it happens to be an open secret—because the stakes are high, and attempts at survival could be jeopardized?

And then, what of me, and my role as a journalist? Can I demand answers when faced with reticence, or probe when the subject is clearly disinclined to share information?

While grappling with these dilemmas, I started acquiring an understanding of how stories must be *heard*. A rigid question-and-answer format doesn't always work. Hesitation, the sounds of silence or gestures can be as truthful and powerful as spoken words. I had to grant these women the freedom to let their stories flow in whatever way or manner they chose.

When I gave women the space to speak, I learnt how each narrative could have interwoven skeins of suffering, trauma, healing, resilience, resistance, struggle, humour and, most of all, individuality.

I learnt that I could not pigeon-hole Kashmiri women. Their voices were multiple and diverse, their personas different. There were women who chose to wear the full hijab. Then, there were those who refused to cover their hair, like this young girl coming from a conservative locality, who enjoyed sporting a close crop and wearing jeans. The voices also included students and media activists, women negotiating dangerous spaces in their everyday routines, women who went to court demanding justice and fought epic battles, women who protested by coming out on the streets, women who suffered sexual violence and are trying to rebuild lives in faraway and difficult mountaineous terrains. And finally, women who gathered me, a complete stranger, in a warm embrace and kissed the top of my head before sharing their most intimate secrets.

Most of all, I saw women who refused to remain victims; who, despite the trauma they lived through, had the faith and courage to echo the songs of the 16th century Kashmiri Muslim poetess, Habba Khatun:

The one who dazzles—have you seen that one?
Upon him look!
A sleepless stream in search of him I run,
A restless brook.
In far off woods, a lonely pine I stood
Till he appeared,
My woodcutter, and came to cut the wood.
His fire I feared,
Yet though he burn my logs, behold, I shine,
My ashes wine![4]

These extraordinary women—whose voices and narratives I have attempted to record as truthfully as I can—make the story of Kashmir as rich as it is.

---

[4]Habba Khatun, 'Lol of the Lonely Pine', translated by Nilla Cram Cook, in Tariq Ali, Hilal Bhatt, Angana P. Chatterji, Habba Khatun, Pankaj Mishra and Arundhati Roy, *Kashmir: The Case for Freedom* (London: Verso, 2011), p. 73. A 'lol', roughly the equivalent of the English 'lyric', was introduced by Habba Khatun to Kashmiri poetry to express one brief thought.

INTRODUCTION
A Brief History of Kashmir

An analysis of any kind within Kashmir must begin with an acknowledgement of its chequered past. This isn't easy, however—for history is seldom static, and in times of conflict is wiped out or entirely rewritten.

While it is commonly believed that Kashmir's troubles began with the Partition, the fact is that the region was on edge from as far back as 1846, when the British, by way of the Treaty of Amritsar, awarded the territories of Kashmir, Jammu and Ladakh to Maharaja Gulab Singh for a token sum of money in 'recognition of his services to the British crown'.[1] Thereafter, for almost a century, the second largest princely state in British India, Jammu and Kashmir, came to be ruled by the Dogras—but given the history of their ascent, the maharajas lacked legitimacy in the eyes of large sections of Kashmiris. In the days to come, Kashmiri Muslims began to feel increasingly marginalized and resentful of the all-powerful maharajas and their perceived anti-Islam bias.

---

[1]Quoted in Shakti Kak, 'The Agrarian System of the Princely State of Jammu and Kashmir', *India's Princely States: People, Princes and Colonialism*, edited by Waltraud Ernst and Biswamoy Pati (Oxford: Routledge, 2007).

By July-August 1931, Kashmir began witnessing waves of internal dissent aimed at overthrowing the Dogras, with Sheikh Abdullah becoming a significant Kashmiri player. In 1946, at the height of India's freedom struggle, Abdullah launched the Quit Kashmir Movement, and demanded that the Treaty of Amritsar be abrogated, and the people of Kashmir be made sovereign entities. He was arrested.

But the agitations could not be quelled. In the spring of 1947, the Poonch jagir, which initially erupted in protest against the Dogras' ruthless taxation system, witnessed a full-fledged revolt against Dogra Maharaja Hari Singh. After a bloody confrontation with the Maharaja's forces, on 24 October 1947, the Poonch rebels declared an Azad (free) Kashmir.

These events are near-contiguous with the dismantling of the British Empire and the creation of two nations—India and Pakistan—both of which had territorial ambitions, and saw value in Kashmir's geography and history. The people of Kashmir had to bear the brunt of the Partition more severely than most—not least because Maharaja Hari Singh, who was in charge of determining the princely state's post-Partition future, kept vacillating over the status of the region and the nation it would owe allegiance to.

In the last days of October 1947, even as the flames of communalism wreaked havoc on the newly created nations, several Pathan tribesmen or lashkars from Pakistan's North-West Frontier captured Muzaffarabad and Poonch. According to some historians, the lashkars rushed into Baramulla at the behest of the dissenting Muslims of Poonch who feared slaughter.[2] The fierce attacks in Baramulla and the imminent

---

[2]See Christopher Snedden, *Kashmir: The Unwritten History* (New Delhi:

threat of the lashkars marching towards Srinagar (barely 56 kilometres away) at last forced Maharaja Hari Singh to act authoritatively. He appealed to India for help, and India, on its part, refused any form of assistance till an Instrument of Accession (to India) was signed by Kashmir. This was done with much haste and was accepted by the then Governor General of India, Lord Louis Mountbatten. On 27 October 1947, soldiers of the first battalion of the Sikh Regiment were airlifted into Srinagar.

Former BBC correspondent, Andrew Whitehead, notes that it is *this* hurried accession by the Maharaja that prevented a clear delineation of the terms and conditions of Kashmir's union with India.[3] He points to Mountbatten's acceptance of accession, which reads:

> It is my government's wish that, as soon as law and order have been restored in Jammu and Kashmir and her soil cleared of the invader, the question of the State's accession should be settled by a reference to the people.[4]

This was a stance echoed by Sheikh Abdullah, too, in a 1948 speech, shortly before he took oath as Jammu and Kashmir's prime minister:

> When the raiders came to our land, massacred thousands of people, mostly Hindus and Sikhs, but Muslims, too— abducted thousands of girls, Hindus, Sikhs and Muslims alike, looted our property and almost reached the gates

---

HarperCollins, 2013).
[3]Andrew Whitehead, *A Mission in Kashmir* (New Delhi: Penguin, 2008).
[4]Also quoted in Humra Quraishi, *Kashmir: The Untold Story* (New Delhi: Penguin, 2004).

of our summer capital, Srinagar, the result was that the civil, military and police administrations failed. [...] We will accept this accession because, without Kashmir's acceding to the Indian dominion, we are not in a position to render any military help. But once the country is free from the raiders, marauders and looters, this accession will be subject to ratification by the people.[5]

Whitehead therefore notes that the accession was provisional or temporary.

Expectedly, the manner of accession was bitterly contested by Pakistan. India maintained that the attack of the tribesmen was engineered by its newly created neighbour in an attempt to override the Maharaja's decision and illegally administer parts of Kashmir. Pakistan, on the other hand, challenged the Instrument of Accession itself, claiming that the Maharaja's consent was not legitimate. Soon after Independence, the respective armies of India and Pakistan were fighting their first battle—often referred to as the First Kashmir War—during which time, Baramulla was recaptured by India. With the intervention of the United Nations (UN), a ceasefire line (CFL)— later known as the line of control (LoC)—took effect in January 1949. It was a line that would go on to rip apart communities and artificially create a Pakistan-administered Kashmir (also known as Azad Kashmir)—which included Muzaffarabad and a part of Poonch—and an India-administered Kashmir.

It is worth remembering that for the early decades, the LoC remained indeterminate. Author Cabeiri deBergh Robinson

---

[5]Excerpts from the Speech by Sheikh Mohammed Abdullah in the UN Security Council Meeting No. 241 held on 5 February 1948, in <http://www.jammu-kashmir.com/documents/abdulun48.html>, accessed on 22 July 2016.

reflects on this 'permeable, often fluid and sometimes irrelevant border'[6]—reminding us that civilians thought it was their right to collect fruit from a tree that lay just beyond a fortified LoC, convinced that they were not the ones trespassing. It was the army patrol that had wandered across the line:

> Many people traversed the lines in the first decades after its establishment. Most of these crossings had nothing, overtly, to do with politics. Villages near the LoC had close links with villages and communities on the other side. Families and social groups were divided across the India- and Pakistan-administered regions, and people continued to reaffirm their kinship ties. Residents of the villages on the line crossed it to attend important ritual events like weddings and funerals. The reinforcement of kinship ties through marriage and the continued participation in exchanges of ritual labour were particularly important for refugees as an expression of their social commitment to the idea of return. Refugees, who thought of themselves as temporarily resettled, sought to reinforce their social networks in the villages from which they had been displaced.[7]

After the 1971 border war between India and Pakistan though, the LoC hardened. Kashmir and its people were divided militarily.

While the two nations view Kashmir through the prism of a territorial dispute, many Kashmiris on both sides of the LoC believe that what they wrestle with is a 'masla-e-Kashmir'—an

---

[6]Cabeiri deBergh Robinson, *Body of a Victim, Body of Warrior: Refugee Families and the Making of Kashmiri Jihadists* (Oakland: University of California Press, 2013).
[7]Ibid.

unfinished Kashmir question—the incomplete realization of their own rights and aspirations of sovereignty. They say the dominant narrative of Kashmir's politics that articulated as India against Pakistan, has excluded their own voices. Over the years, through social media platforms, they have challenged this dominance with the common refrain, *'Yeh mulk hamara hai, iska faisla hum karenge.'* ('This is our land and we will resolve its fate.')

Many Kashmiris also hold that the airlifting of Indian troops into the state, way back in 1947, was the very first step towards militarization, as opposed to political negotiation. By the early 1990s, militarization—or the increasing use of the military as a proxy for governance and as a means to achieve a political objective—only gained in strength, first to fight Pakistan, then to counter the armed struggle for self-determination or azadi helmed by the youth of Kashmir.

◆

This brings us to the word we most commonly associate with Kashmir's struggle—azadi—which, in the nineties, got translated into an armed struggle.

The trigger for this call for freedom was the growing feeling through the decades that there was little room for the democratic process. In August 1953, Sheikh Abdullah's government had been dismissed and he was arrested on charges of treason, probably based on fears that he was rethinking his support for accession. The disenchantment with Indian democracy was heightened with the way Bakshi Ghulam Mohammed, G.M. Sadiq and others—who had once served on Sheikh Abdullah's committee to explore possibilities of a plebiscite—were now part of the government that replaced Abdullah. Their reign of bribery, nepotism and corruption in addition to their role as usurpers alienated even the elite of Kashmir.

Abdullah's release in March 1968 and the subsequent signing of the accord in 1975 with Indira Gandhi would, in later years, be cited as the complete capitulation to India and a loss of honour. Abdullah, once a towering figure, would also be criticized for his authoritarianism and dislike for dissent. It was in 1978 that the draconian Public Safety Act allowing preventive detention was promulgated to quell the waves of dissent.

The final catalyst came with the elections of 1987—believed to have been massively rigged, according to even bureaucrats like Wajahat Habibullah.[8] Contesting in the elections were Abdullah's Jammu and Kashmir National Conference (NC), the Indian National Congress and the Muslim United Front (MUF)—the Jamaat-e-Islami-led conglomerate of anti-National Conference, anti-Congress, pro-plebiscite parties, formed in 1986, that many predicted would fare remarkably well. However, in the run-up to the elections, hundreds of workers from the MUF were beaten and jailed under the Public Safety Act (PSA).[9]

Journalist Tavleen Singh reported, 'In the constituency of Handwara, [...MUF candidate] Abdul Ghani Lone's traditional bastion, as soon as counting began on 26 March, Lone's

---

[8]See Wajahat Habibullah, *My Kashmir: The Dying of the Light* (New Delhi: Penguin, 2011).

[9]'The Public Safety Act gives the Jammu and Kashmir government the power to detain anyone who acts "in any manner prejudicial to the maintenance of public order". To be precise, an individual faces the risk of being detained if he or she is found "promoting, propagating, or attempting to create feelings of enmity or hatred or disharmony on grounds of religion, race, caste and community".' See 'Public Safety Act in Jammu and Kashmir', Elections.in, in <http://www.elections.in/political-corner/public-safety-act-in-jammu-and-kashmir/>, accessed on 22 March 2016.

counting agents were thrown out of the counting station by the police.'[10]. Political scientist Sumantra Bose wrote that when the opponent to the MUF's Muhammad Yusuf Shah, '[was] routed in the contest, [he left] the counting center in a visibly dejected mood and [went] home. But he [was] summoned back—to be declared the winner by presiding officials.'[11]

Such manipulation, widely believed to have been manoeuvred by the Central government to snatch the elections away from the people and retain control over the state's politics,[12] completed the total disenchantment with the Indian democratic system.

According to a few contemporary sociologists, this sense of disillusionment was accompanied by a generational shift in aspirations. Those born in the late 1950s and early 1960s had been the recipients of the material benefits of Sheikh Abdullah's 'Naya Kashmir' manifesto[13] and its dynamic land reforms. Landless peasants, who had come of age hearing stories of forced labour and the injustices of the Dogra kings, suddenly became the proud possessors of land and could hope for social mobility and financial security. This was the 'wushnear' (Kashmiri word that connotes coziness

---

[10]Tavleen Singh, *Kashmir: A Tragedy of Errors* (New Delhi: Penguin, 2000).

[11]Sumantra Bose, *Kashmir: Roots of Conflict, Paths to Peace* (Cambridge: Harvard University Press, 2005).

[12]See Praveen Donthi, 'How Mufti Mohammad Sayeed Shaped the 1987 Elections in Kashmir,' *Caravan*, 23 March 2016.

[13]'The Naya Kashmir Manifesto, as it became known, was adopted by the National Conference in August 1945. It had an inclusive charter for social change with emphasis on equal rights for women, the right to education and the right to work, among other progressive measures. The most radical reform was the abolition of landlordism and the distribution of land to the tiller. [It was] argued that such a progressive agenda could be implemented only by overthrowing the feudal order.' See Shanti Kak, 'Kashmir's Hero', *Frontline*, volume 26, issue 9, 25 April–8 May 2009.

or warmth) generation, one that could 'flirt' with fulfilment. But the generation that followed, that could dream bigger—its goals unhindered by memories of the Dogra subjugation— was doomed to get increasingly restless, explained Arif Ayaz Parrey, a writer and journalist working in Delhi, one of the men I interviewed.

The new and fresh forms of aggression that continued to pile up after the Sheikh's arrest and the way in which Article 370 (which had been promised as a means of supporting Kashmir's unique status) was used as a kind of tunnel to push through a political Sanskritization, was seen as a loss of honour. It was exacerbated by the rigged elections and bid to control the legislature. 'A pervasive sense of loss began to descend upon us. It continues to this day,' said Arif.

With armed revolt being perceived as the only way forward, in the 1990s, hundreds of Kashmiris crossed the border into Pakistan and returned as militants. Prominent among them was Syed Mohammed Yusuf Shah, the one-time MUF candidate of the high-profile Amirakadal constituency, who had been arrested in the counting hall. He took on the name Salahudeen (after the legendary Seljuk Turks), and went on to head the Hizb-ul-Mujahideen (HM).

While the call for azadi in the 1990s had initially been stoked by the Jammu Kashmir Liberation Front (JKLF)— it had advocated complete independence for Kashmir with the cry, *'Kashmir banega khudmuktar'* ('Kashmir will be sovereign')—the HM erupted with the slogan, *'Kashmir banega Pakistan'* ('Kashmir will be a part of Pakistan'). Pakistan's early support for the JKLF swiftly transferred to HM. The JKLF, not only stopped receiving Pakistani aid, but also suffered splits and defections. Finally, in 1994, the JKLF, dreading the elimination of its cadres, called for a ceasefire and took on the role of a political organization (rather than a militant group).

Near-concurrent geopolitical factors also made the conflict increasingly complex. Jihadis from Pakistan, Afghanistan and other nations joined the militancy and operated under outfits like the Harakat-ul-Mujahideen, Jaish-e-Mohammed and Lashkar-e-Taiba. Religious radicals and fidayeens (roughly translated as suicide bombers) carried out fierce attacks.

India's reply to all of this was a massive, no-holds-barred counter-insurgency operation—with enforced disappearances, custodial and extra-judicial killings, torture and sexual violence becoming part of a troubled narrative. This was compounded when Ikhwanis (captured/surrendered militants who turn into pro-government gunmen), nursed by the Indian state, unleashed untold savagery on civilians, practically setting up parallel systems of governance in Kashmir, even while fragmenting communities and creating distrust and suspicion among people. The complete absence of norms and unaccountability defined the bloody years of internecine fighting and counter-fighting.

The most moving and incandescent images of Kashmir's agony during this period have been presented by the iconic poet, the late Agha Shahid Ali. In *The Country Without a Post Office*, guns shoot stars into the sky, towns are left in cinders, and a 'fire that moves on its quick knees' ravages Charar-e-Sharif (caught in a fierce encounter in 1995 between Indian troops and the mujahideen). Agha Shahid Ali's work also speaks of sons 'never to return from the night of torture', mass rapes in villages, bureaucrats driving down streets bereft of children ('they are dead not asleep'), and Pandits fleeing to the plains, clutching Gods from the temples.[14] In one of the most potent epitaphs to the bloody years, the poet concludes: 'They make a desolation and call it peace'.[15]

By the turn of the millennium, around 2003, a shift in geopolitics and the relentless assault of the Indian Army led to a fall in fidayeen attacks and the curtailment of the influx from across the border.[16] Episodes of militancy, too, began tapering off.

But the 'Kashmir problem' was far from solved. Author Arundhati Roy, in a 2008 essay, commented: '[The Indian state] made the mistake of believing that domination was victory, that the "normalcy" it had enforced through the barrel of a gun was indeed normal, and that the people's sullen silence was acquiescence.'[17]

In 2008, armed militancy in the Valley gave way to an

---

[14]19 January is observed as Exodus Day by the Kashmiri Pandits (the Hindu Brahmin minority community) to mark their departure from the Valley in 1995. It is said that between three lakh to four lakh Pandits fled in the nineties, but the exact figures are debatable as Pandits had begun moving out before the armed conflict began because of land reforms. The reasons behind the dramatic exodus on January 1995 are said to be fears of violence and intimidation as anti-Pandit slogans were raised the previous nights. However, the nature of this exodus and the role played by Governor Jagmohan in the mass exit remains contentious. According to J&K Government reports, 219 members of the community were killed in the violence of the nineties and thereafter. Many Pandits who fled were forced to live in camps in Jammu in abject conditions. Siddharth Gigoo is among those who writes poignantly of the exile consciousness. Also read Mridu Rai http://www.aljazeera.com/indepth/spotlight/kashmirtheforgottenconflict/2011/07/2011724204546645823.htm

[15]Agha Shahid Ali, *The Country Without a Post Office* (New York: W.W. Norton & Company, 1998).

[16]See Sumantra Bose, 'The Evolution of Kashmiri Resistance', Al Jazeera, 2 August 2011, in <http://www.aljazeera.com/indepth/spotlight/kashmirtheforgottenconflict/2011/07/2011715143415277754.html>, accessed on 6 April 2016.

[17]Arundhati Roy, 'Azadi', *Outlook*, 1 September 2008.

unarmed mass civil disobedience movement—which asserted itself when civilians took to the streets in the wake of the Amarnath land row and fears of a forced state-engineered demographic change.[18] In 2009, this movement saw a resurgence when the dead bodies of two women, Asiya and Neelofar—believed to have been raped and murdered—were found in the shallow waters of Rambi Ara Nallah near the security camps in Shopian.[19]

By 2010, this unarmed movement had escalated into stark defiance with young boys whipping off their shirts and standing bare-chested in a face-off with the troops. The year also signalled the domination of 'kanni jung' ('a battle with stones') and a steep rise in stone-pelters. Young boys, their faces partially covered with scarves or with hoodies pulled down, targeted bunkers, police posts and armoured vehicles. In his essay, 'Stone Wars', anthropologist and writer Mohamad

---

[18]'[...] the controversial March 5 [2008] order of the state government [transferred] 40 hectares of forest land to the SASB [Shri Amarnath Shrine Board]. [...] The Muslim-dominated Kashmir Valley witnessed violent protests against the transfer of the land to the SASB during the last week. [...] Kashmiris allege the board would settle "outsiders" there and change the demography of the state.' See 'Amaranth Land Row Stir: 70 Protestors Arrested; 9 Injured', *Outlook*, 30 June 2008.

[19]'Those who helped retrieve the bodies of the two women saw enough to suspect that this was a case of rape and murder. [...] When the bodies reached the hospital, there were two post-mortems performed on them to determine the cause of death and any antecedent injuries. It was put out by the police that the deaths were caused by drowning, although the first post-mortem report itself had negated drowning as the cause of death of the two women. [...] six months later, the CBI reportedly claims that what happened that night was a case of drowning. [...] The drowning theory that the CBI is floating does not hold water [...].' See Uma Chakravarty, Usha Ramanathan, Seema Misra, Vrinda Grover, Dr Ajita, Anuradha Bhasin Jamwal, 'Shopian: Manufacturing a Suitable Story', *Independent Women's Initiative for Justice*, in <http://www.countercurrents.org/iwj.pdf>, accessed on 6 April 2016.

Junaid explains the 'battle strategy' and how security troops symbolize Indian domination :

> [...] pelting a stone is purely a political act. Mostly, the stones hit no one. They don't hurt the soldiers, who are always in full body armour, nor are they intended to injure. Stones are thrown from a distance where the stone throwers can outpace soldiers if chased, but this necessary distance also ensures that the stones don't reach the soldiers. They are hurled, as a young man told me, at the 'idea of domination'. They are defiance flying out of hands. Each stone follows its own line of flight out of the hegemonic code. [...]
>
> 'Stone throwing is an art,' a young man explained. The soldiers are not artists, but part of the creation itself. If the streets are canvasses where stone pelters perfect their techniques, soldiers are just olive-coloured blotches symbolizing Indian domination of the region. 'They have turned themselves into objects of our anger,' the young man said.[20]

◆

Much of this seething anger was also being transmuted into a new generation of militancy. When I visited the Valley in 2014, I found a fresh fervour among the youth who spoke with admiration of these militants of south Kashmir, under the leadership of young Burhan Wani, a commander of the Hizbul Mujahideen. His killing in 2016 was to trigger another massive uprising.

---

[20]Mohamad Junaid, 'Stone Wars', *Guernica*, in <https://www.guernicamag.com/features/stone-wars/>, accessed on 6 April 2015.

Senior journalist Purvaiz Bukhari had observed: 'If the year 2010 marked a transition from armed militancy to mass protests, Burhan Wani's[21] arrival on the scene produced a strategic mix of both, reigniting hopes of azadi among many Kashmiris.'

Even as Id celebrations were winding down on the evening of 8 July 2016, news of the killings of Burhan and two other militants, Sartaj Ahmad Sheikh and Parvez, spread. A steady stream of mourners began gathering at Burhan's home village in Tral. The numbers would swell to an estimated two lakh and funeral prayers would be read back to front several times to enable the crowds to view the face of their iconic leader.[22]

The protests that soon snowballed, despite the most violent repression, continued for over two months.

Clearly the state and the J&K Police were caught unawares by the extent of resentment in the Valley and the way Burhan's killing would act as a catalyst, as even former RAW Chief, A.S. Dulat admitted.[23]

Bukhari notes how it is not possible to understand the 'aftermath of the youthful and iconic militant's death without a substantial examination of the intervals of seeming peace, usually marked by a high inflow of tourists, the uneventful conduct of the Amarnath Yatra and the regularly held elections. A genuinely meaningful political engagement with the question of Kashmir never even gets a start.'[24]

He adds how Wani's death 'resonated with everyone

---

[21]http://scroll.in/article/811710/the-rise-of-burhan-and-the-aftermath-of-his-death-show-why-status-quo-in-kashmir-is-unacceptable.

[22]http://www.tribuneindia.com/news/jammu-kashmir/two-lakh-across-valley-attend-burhan-wani-s-funeral/263661.html.

[23]http://thewire.in/61970/kashmir-dulat-interview/.

[24]http://scroll.in/article/811710/the-rise-of-burhan-and-the-aftermath-of-his-death-show-why-status-quo-in-kashmir-is-unacceptable.

affected by death, and the decades of destruction, massacres and rapes, disappearances, torture and trauma that has been the story of Kashmir. When he left home to fight it, he did so not by hiding behind a code name, or crossing over to the Pakistani side of Kashmir for arms and training. He became everyone for whom the prevailing conditions and the status quo was unacceptable.'

In his essay, Mohamad Junaid discounts as naïve the notion that it was personal violence against him and his brother that drew Burhan to militancy. Junaid notes that it was a political maturity that empowered him to see the nature of Indian rule in Kashmir.

'...is it then an accident that Burhan became Commander Burhan Wani? Or is it immanent to a condition of injustice that rebels such as Burhan emerge or the methods they choose?'[25]

Junaid also notes how Burhan Wani's ingenious use of the social media—the images and videos uploaded—created a powerful visual counterculture that was immensely appealing.

'In image after image, and video after video, the young commander was seen not as a figure on the run, but one who seemed to truly enjoy his life among his comrades.'

This visual counterculture of a joyful rebel spurred the 'emergence of the exuberant new movement driven by spontaneous solidarities, and the collective expression of popular sentiment against the forces of occupation.'

A significant feature of the 2016 uprising was that it was not just the youth that poured into the streets. Women, young and old, together with elderly men, lawyers, doctors treating patients were all seen actively participating in the sit-ins or

---

[25]http://raiot.in/the-restored-humanity-of-the-kashmiri-rebel/.

making strong statements about the killing.

Significantly too, support for Kashmiris came from Kargil in the Ladakh region and a shutdown was also observed in the Chenab Valley of Jammu.

◆

According to the government's figures, there are now about 5,00,000-7,00,000 armed personnel in Kashmir. By the state's own admission, militancy is now dramatically reduced. There are perhaps only about 450 militants in the Valley. But the troops remain at a ratio of one soldier to ten civilians.[26]

There are three significant facets to militarization in Kashmir. Researcher Seema Kazi, while analyzing the build-up of militarization in the Valley, suggests that what complicates the narrative in the region is that the people's struggle against 'occupation' is conflated with matters of national defence. She says:

> The construction of Kashmir's revolt as a threat to 'the nation' legitimized a violent nation-state building exercise in Kashmir even as the Indian state's representation of Kashmir as a Pakistan instigated conspiracy reduced Kashmir's struggle against state tyranny to an issue of 'national' territorial defence. This inside/outside duality transformed Kashmir into the most heavily militarized region in the world.[27]

---

[26]Gautam Navlakha, 'The False God of Military Suppression', *Until My Freedom Has Come*, edited by Sanjay Kak (New Delhi: Penguin, 2011).
[27]Seema Kazi, *Between Democracy and Nation: Gender And Militarisation in Kashmir* (New Delhi: Women Unlimited, 2008). Also see the author's thesis on the same subject in <http://etheses.lse.ac.uk/2018/1/U501665.pdf>, 2007, accessed on 21 March 2016.

The second significant aspect of militarization in the Valley is the manner in which the army has nurtured Ikhwanis—thus remaining 'unaccountable for the cycle of anonymous killings executed under its patronage and tutelage'.[28] Journalist Sudha Ramachandran notes:

> Not only did the [Ikhwanis] train their guns on the militants but they did so against unarmed civilians as well. They were brutal in their methods to elicit information from the locals. They used their weapons to fight the militancy but gradually used these to settle personal scores, to extort and to further their individual interests. [...] The terror unleashed by the Ikhwanis has been so serious that many Kashmiris say they fear them more than they do the militants or the security forces.[29]

When Ikhwanis were stripped of their official cover in 1998, it led to another cycle of blood-letting—with the once-invincible renegades and their families getting exposed to the wrath of unforgiving militants.

Finally, while the military has been granted the power to repress dissidence, it has also been accompanied by extraordinary security legislation which provides a blanket of immunity against crimes like unlawful detentions, torture, custodial deaths and even rapes. The Armed Forces (Special Powers) Act (AFSPA) 1990, which is also in force in parts of the northeast, empowers troops to search and arrest citizens without warrants, shoot unarmed civilians, even if it is with the intent to kill, and raid houses or destroy any

---

[28]Ibid.

[29]Sudha Ramachandran, 'The Downside to India's Kashmir "Friendlies",'*Asia Times Online*, in <http://www.atimes.com/atimes/South_Asia/EI26Df07. html>, 26 September 2003, accessed on 22 July 2016.

property that is 'likely' to be used by insurgents. Further, it stipulates that there can be no prosecution or any other legal proceeding against such troops without sanction from the Central government.

Although applications have been made to prosecute alleged perpetrators of crime in a number of cases, not a single sanction has been given since its imposition.[30] The climate of an all-pervasive immunity means that even the normal procedures of ordinary criminal law (like registering an FIR, initiating investigations or filing a closure report before a magistrate) are likely to be disregarded, and indeed, have been.

What we see emerging is a Kafkaesque universe—and it is against this backdrop that we must understand the position of women and children in Kashmir.

---

[30]Sudha Ramachandran, 'India's Controversial Armed Forces (Special Powers) Act', *The Diplomat*, in <http://thediplomat.com/2015/07/indias-controversial-armed-forces-special-powers-act/>, 2 July 2015, accessed on 22 March 2016.

Chapter One

A SOLDIER UNDER A CHINAR
Navigating Kashmir's Morphed Landscape

One cold November afternoon, as my Kashmiri friends and I were returning to Srinagar, my attention was drawn to two women walking across a field. Simply clad in pherans,[1] with baskets placed on their heads, they looked around warily and then faded into a greying horizon. A soldier in full gear—battle fatigues, a helmet, boots and a rifle—watched them intently from his position under a chinar tree.

The sheer incongruity of the scene left me wondering aloud: What do women feel about the presence of strangers holding guns and grenades, in their own fields and orchards? And, that these strangers have the right to use their weapons with impunity? What is it like to work and function under this hostile male scrutiny every single day, all the time?

Even as I pointed to the soldier under the chinar tree, my friends cried out in alarm, 'Do you want us to get shot? You simply cannot do this in Kashmir!' A little later, when frayed nerves had been calmed, one of my friends explained that this

---

[1] A pheran is a long coat or cloak made of wool or tweed, worn both by women and men in the Valley.

was a reality that Kashmiris had lived with for more than two decades. They had to contend with not only the physical presence of the military, but also the process of militarization.

I remembered this episode three years later, on a warm May morning, when another scene unfolded, at odds with the preceding one. I was standing next to 'Pestonjee's white horse'—a big wooden horse statue in Srinagar's prominent shopping arcade. There were several sightseers and security troops—many of whom were accompanying government or army officials on shopping expeditions.

Suddenly, a smartly dressed Indian lady tourist in trousers and coat, with a little boy in tow, strode towards some of the troops and greeted them with confidence and ease. Tapping one of them on the arm, she said, 'My son wants to say hello. He is pestering me for a gun just like yours. He asks, "Why do so many men have guns?"' The Kashmiri policeman laughed in response and said, *'Yeh toh Kashmir hai na!'* ('This is Kashmir, after all.')

I was struck by the schism in the approach of this tourist and the Kashmiri women I had seen walking past the chinar tree and their divergent ways of looking at things.

For most Kashmiris, the massive deployment of security troops and the presence of armed policemen around, is 'occupation'.[2] For most Indians the presence of the military and the police within the Valley is normal, even reassuring—a way of preserving national unity and security, and a means of countering the 'destabilizing' forces behind Kashmir's freedom struggle.

---

[2]Refer to E. Benvenisti, *The International Law of Occupation*, Oxford University Press or A. Roberts, 'Transformative Military Occupation: Applying the Laws of War and Human Rights', American Journal of International Law.

◆

How does one understand Kashmir and its sense of pervading loss? How has militarization transformed its landscape and eroded its cultural matrix? One way of imagining Kashmir, as it once was, is through Habba Khatun and what she symbolizes for the people, especially women. This mystic wanderer and poet is cherished by Kashmir's women partly because her biography resonates with them. Trapped in a loveless marriage and in a family that poured scorn on her literary aspirations, Habba Khatun dared to break free and fall in love with Yousuf Shah Chak, Kashmir's ruler.

But her joy was short-lived, for Yousuf Shah was soon imprisoned by the Mughals. Habba Khatun's life, thereafter, became a tale of yearning. Her search for the missing fragment of a half-fulfilled dream is a part of Kashmir's unconscious.

If Habba Khatun is loved, it is also because her poems are a reminder of a life once familiar in Kashmir—her verses are replete with allusions to wandering in open spaces, gathering wild basil or jasmine flowers, or drawing water from the wells. One poem reads: *'Gather violets, O Narcissus/Winter's ashes from our doors I fling!/The water bird the lake embraces/How can frost upon your petals cling?'*[3]

In Habba Khatun's verses, there lives a time when groups of girls could pick chinar leaves and twist them into ornaments, or walk into forests to collect firewood, or celebrate the coming of spring in *badamwaris*.

It was senior psychiatrist, Dr Arshad Hussain at the mental health hospital in Rainawari who first spoke of the loss of

---

[3]Habba Khatun, 'Gather Violets, O Narcissus', translated by Nilla Cram Cook, in Tariq Ali, Hilal Bhatt, Angana P. Chatterji, Habba Khatun, Pankaj Mishra and Arundhati Roy, *Kashmir: The Case for Freedom* (London: Verso, 2011), p. 74.

traditional spaces. He explained how the very area around us was once a large *badamwari*—stretching across a thousand 'kanals'. It was a space where families would flock after the end of a harsh winter: or where they would have picnics with, white sheets spread out to hold nun-chai;[4] or where jugglers and magicians and vendors selling water chestnuts would gather. Today, this erstwhile badamwari has given way to concrete colonies. Others have been taken over by the army.

Also lost are traditional *yaarbals* or washing ghats where women would assemble at midday, not just to wash clothes but talk. Dr Arshad pointed out how these shared spaces of conversation, where worries were aired, were also spaces of abreaction (free expression and consequently release of suppressed emotions). Yaarbals disappeared largely because of the violence of the conflict and increasing urbanization.

◆

Indeed, the insidious process of militarization has almost completely altered the fabled landscape of Jammu and Kashmir—with over 600 security force camps occupying 3.5 lakh acres of land[5]. Military infrastructure and firing grounds dominate mountain highlands and forests, karewas (or plateaus of glacial deposits) and alpine lands, paddy fields and glaciers. The jackboots have left deep imprints. Concertina wire, bunkers and troops in armoured cars are as ubiquitous as the ancient chinars.

It is impossible for even the most casual of visitors to miss

---

[4]Also known as pink tea, nun-chai, one of Kashmir's most popular beverages, is known for its salty aftertaste.
[5]Figure is taken from Gautam Navlakha's essay, 'The False God of Military Suppression' in the book *Until My Freedom Has Come* edited by Sanjay Kak (p. 163)

the signs of occupation or capture spaces bereft of symbols of combat. I remember a summer afternoon when, walking across the ootwalli (camel's back) bridge at Amira Kadal, I attempted photographing fisherwomen with their baskets of fish as ravenous eagles hovered overhead. Loops of twisted wire kept intruding and disturbing the composition from whichever angle I tried to click. Finally, I took comfort in the wild yellow flowers that forced their way through those metal coils, brazenly disregarding the rules of the land.

Kashmir's menacing material environment of sandbags, barricades, checkpoints and fencing has had a profound impact on its people. It has dramatically altered mental mappings. A woman whom I had met in my early days in the Valley, told me with regret, 'These symbols of occupation are now so entrenched in our psyche that we unconsciously use them as markers for directions. If I have to guide a stranger, I no longer refer to tree-lined avenues or ancient houses as signposts. I say, turn left at the CRPF camp, go towards the checkpost, and turn right near the bunker.'

The average Kashmiri's disconnect with the landscape is heightened by the way buildings, heritage structures and landmarks have been appropriated and used for counter-insurgency purposes. In downtown Srinagar, former cinema houses, a few hotels and heritage buildings now serve as makeshift security camps and lie swaddled in nets and wire.

The Hari Niwas Palace, once the striking residence of the former maharaja and now a state guest house, comes with chilling associations for Samreen Mushtaq. For this young researcher—who lost her father when she was just three years old and later learnt of his custodial killing through a newspaper clipping, the Hari Niwas Palace will always be the infamous interrogation centre, the site of torture and extrajudicial killings.

Whenever she goes past the Palace, Samreen says she is haunted by unsettling thoughts about what happened to her father and thousands of others who now lie in unknown graves.

In the eyes of its residents, Kashmir, once eulogized by poets for its unparalleled loveliness—has morphed into a bleak land of desolation. Military hoof-marks not only connote a loss of space but also liberties. 'I feel caged,' is one of the commonest refrains. Given the frequency of curfews, crackdowns, shootouts, shutdowns, encounters, mass arrests, street protests and firing, plans or commitments remain conditional. It is dependent on the 'haalat' ('the situation'). In Kashmir, *'haalat dekh kar'* (after assessing the scene) is all-too-common an expression.

◆

Aliya Bashir, a young journalist, who lived in downtown Srinagar until she recently married, recalled what it is like to live in close proximity to a militarized world.

'The main door was six footsteps away from the CRPF camp and the men could be seen everywhere. My sister's room was directly opposite. She did not want even a tiny speck of light to be visible to the men outside and so kept the three iron-grilled windows closed and the curtains drawn all the time. She avoided spending much time in that "dark room"as we called it. It felt unsafe, especially on Fridays and Sundays—because of the protests and stone-pelting that invariably happened on the streets. The CRPF too hurl stones and our windows were in the line of action. We were always sitting in fear wondering when they would get smashed. At other times, we thought we would never be free of the nauseating smell of tear gas.'

Living in downtown Srinagar also made it challenging for Aliya to pursue her career. In February 2013, even as an extensive 'safety net' enveloped Kashmir to forestall protests against Afzal Guru's execution, Aliya had to meet her editor visiting from California. 'Somehow, I summoned up the courage to tell my mother that I had to step out of the house and proceed to Lal Chowk. She was livid. While I could appreciate her anxiety—after all, just a few days earlier, a local journalist had been brutally beaten up by security forces for daring to venture out on the streets—I had my career to think of. Finally, I was allowed to step out—but I had my mother, uncle and aunt accompanying me all the way to the police station. After that, I was on my own.

'As I walked down, I was time and again asked to produce my identity card. A policeman mocked my choice of profession, and tried to intimidate me. "What are you going to write about, us?" he asked. "Will you be writing against us?" I refused to argue with him, and was finally allowed to go. After the meeting, I walked all the way back from Lal Chowk, past CRPF men patrolling the old city, past troops gazing at me and passing comments. I tried to ignore them all. Once home, I refused to speak of my day. If my mother knew what all I had to endure, she would never again allow me to leave the house.

◆

A culturescape is now being instated to defy cold, metallic warscapes. Once-prominent (and now appropriated) landmarks carry swirls of graffiti. 'Go India, go back', the most visible slogan of 2010, continues to be scratched across walls, pavements and streets. In the ongoing propaganda war this catchphrase is sometimes stealthily replaced by 'good'.

In downtown Srinagar, the letters 'A-z-a-d-i' slide vertically down an electricity pole. On newly constructed flyovers, one spies painted slogans that align local struggles with global movements—'Save Gaza' is juxtaposed with calls for Kashmiri freedom.

Government buildings near Peerzoo Island and along Srinagar's Bund (facing the River Jhelum) are locally referred to as 'Peerzoo Gallery'. As a manifestation of a burgeoning hip-hop subculture, walls carry spray-painted declarations: 'Revolution is loading'; 'Capitalism is crisis'; and 'PSA zone'—a clever use of irony directed at the Public Safety Act.

The pervasive milieu of militarization has also profoundly affected a new generation of designers. Mahum Shabir, who feels estranged from traditional, placid Kashmiri motifs like chinar leaves and flowers, has now set up an online shawl business, with fellow designer and artist Suhail Mir. The shawls in which barbed wires are used as recurring motifs and paisleys are in a face-off with Kalashnikovs, that represent the true spirit of the times, say the designers and are reflective of the way in which the conflict is now a part of Kashmir's collective psyche.

◆

In order to really understand Kashmir's socio-political and cultural psyche, one must move out from the typical tourist sites of the Dal Lake and the gardens and go into downtown Srinagar. My friend Ifrah Reshi, from this vicinity, helped me to explore its web of lanes—the city's innards, as it were. My mind reeled with the impressions—Jamia and Pathar Masjids, shrines like Bulbul Lankar, old buildings with Kashmiri architectural flourishes, shops with wicker ware and samovars, bridges or kadals that spanned the Jhelum and cemeteries including the Mazar-e-Shuhada (martyrs' graveyard).

Downtown Srinagar was also where resistance was alive and, according to Ifrah, thriving because of the area's layout—a warren of streets that one could weave in and out of, a place with 'Open Sesame' doors that magically open to offer refuge to fleeing stone–pelters and others. Ifrah recalled a time when she was out buying stationery and a cordon was thrown around the lanes of her home while security troops chased a few boys. Ifrah, darted into a neighbourhood shop in one of the narrow alleyways and stayed there till things quietened down. This, she said, was common practice. Even young schoolgirls, out for tuition classes, would often hide in one of the tucked-away homes or eateries if the 'haalat' turned bad.

Author Mohamad Junaid, writing on spaces of occupation observes:

> If the security grid that models the occupation of space defamiliarizes ordinary places like main road, avenues, public squares, parks and so on, intense socio-political activity takes place in the inner cities, downtowns, narrow lanes, cramped crevasses deep in mohallas, street corner shop fronts and small non-descript tea stalls. The occupation of space is answered through the occupation of places.[6]

In the same essay, Junaid adds: 'Amid occupation's deeply spatial character resistance recovers a sense of place, for

---

[6]Mohamad Junaid, 'Life and Death Under Occupation', *Everyday Occupations: Experiencing Militarism in South Asia and the Middle East*, edited by Kamala Visweswaran (Pennsylvania: University of Pennsylvania Press, 2013), p. 177.

instance, by continuing everyday life despite the difficulties and obstacles produced by occupation, or by adjusting social life instead of letting it fragment.'[7] This, too, rings true when one considers how the plan of downtown Srinagar—the way buildings are sited in close proximity—has fostered a strong sense of community. Women, who may be unable to step outside, make use of windows to gain access to outdoor happenings. Animated conversations across dwellings—or what a young girl referred to as 'window talk'—happen all the time. Be it news of protests, rallies or funeral processions, they are all conveyed through these often elegant openings to a wider world.

On the flipside, windows have also let in violence. Fancy Jan was killed with a bullet when she went to draw the curtains of her home.[8]

Often the acrid smoke of tear-gas shells or chilli grenades[9] permeates the house the moment windows are opened. Uzma Qureishi, a social worker, told me, 'At such times, you feel as if your throat is on fire. You cough and cough and cough for hours together.'

◆

Even as Kashmir remains a tortured land, its children have

---

[7]Ibid.
[8]Sanjay Kak, 'The Last Option: A Stone in Her Hand', *The Times of India*, 8 August 2010.
[9]Chilli grenades, developed by the DRDO (Defence Research and Development Organization), contain the world's hottest chillies, known as bhut jolokia. When these grenades are used, their ingredients are released into the air. Amnesty International has criticized the use of chilli grenades. See 'Indian Army Develops Blinding Chili Grenade', *Fox News*, in <http://www.foxnews.com/tech/2010/03/19/indian-army-unveils-blinding-chili-grenade.html>, 19 March 2010, accessed on 15 July 2016.

to pay a horrendous price if they navigate spaces with impulsiveness or curiosity. Nayeem Rather discovered how the ephemeral joys of childhood like a school picnic could be blown into shards.

Nayeem was among the group of friends I had been introduced to on one of my first few visits to Anantnag (or Islamabad, as many Kashmiris call it).

After lunch at a restaurant, Nayeem was washing his hands as I waited for my turn near the sink. Earlier, while having my meal, I had noticed how, despite a missing thumb and a huge wad of misshapen tissue, he had still managed to use the affected hand with dexterity. As he turned around at the sink, he asked me cheerfully, 'Are you looking at my hand? That's a memento I got years ago from a picnic.'

Two months later, at Srinagar's charmingly named Hollywood Café, Nayeem—I learnt he was a journalist— recounted the story of his missing thumb with a touching combination of attentiveness and humour. 'I remember it all so clearly,' he said, '4 July 2002, I was ten years old, studying in Class V and our school had taken us to Sonamarg for a picnic. We played around near the Thajiwas Glacier, close to the army camp when one of the boys spotted a cylindrical-shaped metallic object that had us fascinated. We started looking around for more such objects that were lying scattered between the bushes and trees and started stuffing them into our pockets—oblivious of the fact that these could be unexploded devices.'

Nayeem continued, 'An hour-and-a-half later I discovered a bright blue object with a protrusion at one end that, to my childish eyes, seemed like a rolling pin. I was most excited and curious about my find and wanted to show it off to my friends. I sat on my haunches and struck it on the ground.

Suddenly there was a huge explosion and we fell to the ground with the impact. I clearly remember seeing the exposed bone of my hand and blood gushing out and the green fields through which I ran seeking help. Later I learnt the object was a flare used to light up the area.'

Nayeem was taken to a local dispensary, and from there—with considerable difficulty, for there was no ambulance in the region, and only an Ambassador car with a malfunctioning brake—transferred to a bone and joint hospital in Barzulla. He was later shifted to SKIMS—where he was placed under the care of noted plastic surgeon Dr Shabir Iqbal. Nayeem recalled, 'Dr Iqbal asked me what I had picked from the ground, and I innocently replied, "F-16"—without knowing what it really meant—that F-16s were, in fact, fighter planes. I only knew that news channels kept flashing these letters on the screen those days. And he laughed adding,"Even today, when I meet Dr Iqbal, he calls me F-16.

'Before the operation could take place, there was another nerve-wracking exercise since my pockets were stuffed with shells. The police actually had to be called to handle these souvenirs of mine.'

Nayeem spent forty days in hospital. His recollections of his special ward for plastic surgery offer a glimpse into the surreal world of a militarized state—where spaces suddenly intersect. 'There was a militant from Islamabad (Anantnag),' Nayeem told me, 'who had been injured in a razed building. Then, there was also a young woman, recovering from a cleft palate surgery. The two fell in love, even as a major from Ganderbal, a double amputee, and I watched. Their story became the talk of the hospital!'

It was the odd coming together of a militant, an army man and civilians, of the merger of distinct geographies. And it was disturbing that this injured youth's story was commonplace. As were glaciers populated with shells. Nayeem, who is from Budgam, actively campaigned to have the army vacate Tos Maidan. A magnificent meadow and a former grazing ground in Budgam, Tos Maidan from 1964 onwards, had become a firing range and a centre for artillery drills. Over the years, sixty-three people lost their lives to undetonated shells, with many others getting disabled. Several of the victims have been children. After a sustained campaign, Tos Maidan was vacated by the Indian Army in 2014 and the grounds turned into a tourist site[10].

But there is little cause for celebration. As long as Kashmir remains militarized, the army will continue to violate its pristine natural expanses.

For me, what is distressing is not only the vanishing of spaces of recreation but that violence has intruded on childhoods—a time that should be kept inviolate. This was brought home most powerfully during the horrific killings of 3 November 2014—which illustrated how simple outings could turn into major tragedies. Five boys set out to see a Muharram procession in the Chattergam Chadoora area (30 kilometres from Srinagar) and the trip ended with a ghastly image, carried by newspapers, of a car with blood dripping down its sides. Two boys dead. Two seriously injured. One (Basim Amin) traumatized.

Soldiers of the 53 Rashtriya Rifles had pumped bullets into the car that had swerved into an electric pole. In a newspaper interview, Amin recalled the moment of horror:

---

[10]http://www.business-standard.com/article/pti-stories/kashmir-s-tosa-maidan-thrown-open-to-public-116052900643_1.html

When the firing stopped after less than a minute, I looked at Faisal who was drenched in blood and not moving. I looked behind and found Mehraj, Shakir and Zahid fallen on each other with blood oozing out from their bodies.[11]

The soldiers claimed that they mistook the teens in the car for terrorists since they had failed to stop at two checkpoints. The story was refuted by the wounded boys and the sole survivor. Later, the army reportedly 'admitted that excessive firing could have been avoided.'[12]

Militarization has not only taken a toll on lives but has also impacted a fragile ecology. A path-breaking report, *Occupational Hazard,*[13] brought out in 2015 by the Jammu Kashmir Coalition of Civil Society (JKCCS) details the ecological damage caused by occupation; it marshals evidence to prove that the catastrophic floods of September 2014 were not 'natural' but a product of militarized governance in highly environmentally sensitive zones. It seems, nature too is in revolt.

Over the years, I have made several journeys to Kashmir and have seen the myriad ways in which its pristine lands have been ravaged and of the terrible violence meted out to its people.

I have come to realize that Kashmir is no place for picnics— not as long as it remains occupied. Not as long as there is a soldier under the chinar.

---

[11]'Budgam Firing: 14-Year-Old Survivor Recalls Horror, Indiscriminate Firing by Army', *DNA*, 7 November 2014.
[12]Toufiq Rashid, '9 Soldiers Indicted for Budgam Shooting', *Hindustan Times*, 27 November 2014.
[13]See *Occupational Hazard: The Jammu and Kashmir Flood of September 2014*, in <http://www.jkccs.net/wp-content/uploads/2015/04/Occupation-Hazard-JKCCS.pdf>, accessed in 14 July 2016.

Chapter Two

JOSH THA, JAWAN THAY
Women's Call for Azadi in the 1990s

One morning, a few kilometres from Anantnag/Islamabad, in school teacher Mubeena's home, I woke up to loud shouts outside eclipsing the gentle chirrup of birds. When I mentioned this to Arif, Mubeena's son, over breakfast of nun-chai and Kashmiri breads, he told me that what I had heard was the battle cry of soldiers conducting morning exercises in a camp closeby.

I smiled sheepishly and turned to Mubeena, who in a splendid gesture of *mehman navazi* (hospitality) had taken leave from her duties in a government school to spend time with me. Mubeena, who would later recount life in the nineties, began on a nostalgic note. She spoke of the time when the nights in Kashmir held no terror; when women could luxuriate in solitary splendour, or enjoy moonlit walks with samovars[14] in their hands bringing tea to those labouring in the fields; a time when women could nonchalantly roll up their salwars to their knees as they worked in their kitchen gardens, when they could commune freely with one another

---

[14]A samovar is an ornate metal container traditionally used to heat water or tea.

and when they were free to return home at any time they wished, even well after 11 p.m.

The magic of moonlight was replaced by nightmares as the nights turned menacing with the nineties.

◆

It was, more precisely, in 1988–89—that a whole generation of Kashmiris, disillusioned with India's 'broken promises' and electoral politics, crossed its borders and returned as armed militants. In the early 1990s, the popular imagination of Kashmir—fired as it was by dreams of freedom through militancy—was marked by passion or 'jazbaa'—a highpoint of emotion that has not quite been matched since. The sound of Kalashnikovs wielded by militants was in sync with the full-throated cries of 'azadi' from the huge crowds that spilled into the streets. Songs like 'Jago, jago, subah ayee' ('awake, awake, the morning has come') inspired people to believe they were at the cusp of a new tomorrow.

During this period, militants were idealized, welcomed everywhere and seen as heroes—to the extent that their outfits became quite the fashion statement. Meenu, a woman from Anantnag/Islamabad, told me that back then, her young brother Nasir had to be physically restrained from hurling himself into the Jhelum—the river that flows between India and Pakistan. In his childish enthusiasm, Nasir thought that its currents would carry him straight into the arms of the militants with whom he felt a sense of solidarity.

Human rights activist and writer Zahir ud Din narrated to me a similar anecdote. A young man, he said, tried (unsuccessfully) to impersonate the JKLF commander Sheikh Abdul Hameed and flirt with a nurse, hoping to reap benefits of the adulation that Kashmiris heaped on the militant! Zahir ud Din, with a wry smile , explained that such was the passion, the 'madness' of the nineties. Among the contributors to the madness of the nineties or what was commonly called the tehreek (movement) was Anjum Zamrud Habib of the Muslim Khawateen Markaz (MKM), a women's outfit, that now falls under the umbrella of the All Party Hurriyat Conference.

At her home in Parraypora, Zamrud outlined the history of the MKM that was founded in 1990 by Bakhtawar Behenji, Nuzwat Rawanda (popularly known as Nunsie), Mehjabeen Akhter, Masooda Qureshi, Mehmooda Baji, Meena Rawanda, Bilquis Mir and Zamrud herself.

Elaborating on the josh (zeal) that defined the nineties, she said, 'We were absolutely committed to the ideal of azadi. We threw ourselves into the struggle. *Bina kissi siyasat se iss field mein the.* (We were out there without any political designs).'

Zamrud's commitment to making women a part of the decision-making narrative came to the fore well before the turbulent nineties, when, as a college-student, she brought together her classmates and raised her voice in protest against the quality of food in her hostel.

Later, as a lecturer at Haneefa College, when she heard of a dowry death in the region, she decided to act: 'My friends and I were sitting on the lawns when news trickled in. As a group, we felt strongly about issues such as women empowerment, and were impelled to do something—even though, at that time, we weren't certain what we *could* do'.

Zamrud and her friends decided to start an awareness drive and hold a meeting of students, teachers, other like-minded women and even those unemployed. They even sought the involvement of the Kashmiri Pandit community which was directly impacted by dowry harassment. 'We managed to bring in two hundred members in a single week.

Every lane that I walked through brought forth women eager to participate. In 1989, we formally registered the Women's Welfare Association and began charging a sum of 50 rupees for membership.'

But the fight for azadi meant that gender issues had to take a backseat and Zamrud threw all her energies in organizing women with the MKM. Like Asiya Andrabi who heads the radical Islamic organization, Duktaran-e-Millat, Zamrud is clear that they did not advocate that women actually pick up the gun but participate in different ways like honing their skills in nursing (the MKM trained women in this field) and by urging them to get involved in demonstrations. Zamrud believed this is where the MKM's strength lay—it coud reach out to the families of those martyred, mobilize thousands of women and get them to actively resist. 'That was our biggest weapon. Clearly women were not useen or unheard then.'

A case in point was in March 1990, when women—at the forefront of dissent—hurled *kangris*[15] at troops outside a stadium in Anantnag/Islamabad—where young boys, picked up during a crackdown, had been detained. 'I was also picked up and labelled as a woman whose home was frequented by militants,' Zamrud said. 'But the security troops let me go and then denied having held me when a call was made to the deputy commissioner of police.'

Acknowledging the contribution of women as a powerful force in the struggle for azadi in 1990s, Zahir ud Din spoke of how a former Border Security Force (BSF) commander had told him that the difference between handling militancy in Kashmir and Punjab was that in Kashmir the troops always had to

---

[15]Kangris are earthen pots with coal embers that Kashmiris use to keep warm in winter.

factor in the huge numbers of women who would confront armed guards on the streets whenever an announcement was made from the mosque.

Zahir ud Din went on to recollect how his neighbourhood, Magarmal Bagh Chowk in Srinagar, used to be viewed as a 'liberated area' up until 1994. Almost every day, there would be demonstrations, with women out in full force and security troops resorting to lathi charge.

Nasir Patigaru of Anantnag/Islamabad also recalled how during his childhood when the army would conduct raids and detain dozens of boys, the women of the locality would march into their camps and shout slogans—a practice they continued until the violence increased so significantly that they were forced to back down.

Besides vociferously rebelling, Kashmiri women began evolving a language of resistance reinforced by humour. Uzma Falak, a writer and filmmaker who I interviewed extensively, recalled: 'The troops couldn't understand Kashmiri, so women would make snide remarks or bait them with jokes. I heard accounts of how troops would be greeted with 'murga chor (chicken thief)—they had a reputation for stealing poultry— and it would freak them out. Yes, women could mobilize themselves and fight back with wit, despite all the surveillance.'

Not only were Kashmiri women demanding azadi, many were also actively supporting the militancy. 'We cooked for them,' Zamrud revealed, 'washed their clothes, ferried supplies and provided logistical help. We could even chide them if we disagreed on something; kareebi rishta, tha (our ties were close).' Women acted as couriers for militants and conveyed vital information—roles that came with grave repercussions. But Josh tha, jawan thay!' ('We were passionate, we were young!') was how she managed to shrug off many dangerous consequences.

During crackdowns and cordon-and-search operations men would be compelled to gather in the streets or in the fields. Women, left alone, would have to deal with military personnel hunting for concealed weapons or militants in their homes. 'There would be frequent searches,' Zamrud told me. 'The troops wanted to know why we were storing large supplies of rice, salt, sugar or dried vegetables. Were we stockpiling essentials in preparation for a war, they would ask us.'

Mubeena also narrated how crackdowns were particularly intensive in 1991. The slow build-up of a military matrix meant that her village came to be surrounded by camps on all four sides that would take turns to raid the homes. 'They would ask us where the militants were holed up, vandalize the kitchen, turn storage bins and jars upside down, smash utensils and leave a trail of strewn spices and grains behind them. We, as teachers, would discuss this in our school. One day, we decided to protest in our own way. I, and others like me, refused to clear the mess on the floor after a bunch of soldiers left. The next night, when another group of security men came in and asked us what happened, I told them that this was the handiwork of their fellow soldiers. They were free to inspect the damage, I added. I was not going to clean up.'

Kashmiri women also had to bear the abusive behaviour of troops along with the men. Mubeena recalled, with agony, the day her husband and other men of the village were taken to the banks of a mountain-stream and flogged until the 'last traces of self-respect were rinsed out' (in the words of her son, Arif, who wrote a poem dedicated to his mother).

During this beating, Mubeena was subjected to abuse and taunts. 'I was told that I was receiving a salary from the government and people like me had no right to think of azadi. When my husband was brought back with injuries on his back, I was told, 'Here is your azadi!'

◆

This overwhelming participation of Kashmiri women in the azadi struggle and their resistance, however, did not translate into political space as Zamrud regretted. Women still do not get these spaces, she added.

At first, she had believed that it was possible to interweave gender concerns and the movement for azadi but later developments proved her wrong. 'In 1993, the Hurriyat had given a call for all social and religious organizations to come under one umbrella. The MKM responded and I assumed that women would continue being involved with decision-making—but the fact is that we were not given that chance.'

While Zamrud maintained that she respected the Hurriyat, she could not get the executive members to understand that giving women space in the fight for self-determination would only bring more vibrancy to the movement; that women had the innate capacity to rebuild fractured societies; that they could add gentleness to the tehreek. Most of all she could not get them to see that 'women represent more than fifty per cent of the population and if they are denied a voice it amounts to denying freedom to more than fifty per cent of the inhabitants of the place.' Nor could she make them realize that the feminist movement and the struggle for azadi could not be delinked.

◆

'I gave my son to azadi.' What did one mean by that? A small remark by a poor woman in Shopian prodded me to try and understand the role of Kashmiri women, who contributed to the decade's fervour, by 'giving up' their sons to the militancy and remained proud of the 'ultimate sacrifice' of their young warriors.

I was welcomed by Misra in her small and very sparsely furnished home. She was, she said, the proud mother of Tariq Ahmad Shah, a young militant who had been killed by security forces in Kellar in 1993. Another son had been mentally challenged and died of natural causes in 2010. As we sat, she almost immediately began talking about Tariq. Her voice turned warm and she said, 'This boy of mine, he was only seventeen when he crossed the border with his friends. He was martyred shortly after he returned.' Misra went on to add, 'Back then, the prevailing sentiment in society was that families with three or more sons should be willing to make a sacrifice for the cause of azadi.'

Misra was unable to articulate her feelings and views any further, but her remark triggered in me the need to understand the sentiments of mothers who, not only accepted the decision of their sons to join the armed movement, but also felt a surge of pride when they were 'martyred'. It became incumbent on me to delve into such fraught subjects as the making of *mujahids* (warriors), the definition of a *shahid* (martyr) and the Islamic struggle for justice—all of which are pivotal to understanding the women's response to their offspring's involvement with Kashmir's fight for self-determination.

Historically, the systems and structures that developed with the spread of Islam have hinged around a duty (*farz*) to fight an injustice (*zulm*). The root of the word zulm comes from the Arabic *zulla* which means to move something from its rightful place. Those who fight zulm accept in the spirit of sacrifice, any harm that might come to them and that others might suffer during the struggle.

Cabeiri deBergh Robinson, who spent many years on both sides of the border studying the Kashmir conflict, refutes the notion that for the Kashmiri fighters, jihad is a collective fight to establish an Islamic polity. She quoted the case of Shafiq, a young man whose father, having been displaced during the 1965 Indo-Pak war from Handwara had come to 'Azad Kashmir.' He said he joined the Kashmir struggle because it was his farz as a Muslim to protect the rights of the oppressed.

Shafiq spoke always in very personal, even intimate terms, about the violation of houses, families and bodies. He neither invoked scriptural references nor referred to religious leaders [...] Instead, he concluded that the struggle was [...] one in which he had a duty to participate, based on his own knowledge of the conditions of violence under which people in border villages lived in the 1990s. For him, the threat that necessitated [this struggle] was not the violation of the sovereign territory (dar) of Islam but the violation of the rights (haque) of Kashmiri people and the bodies of Kashmiri women.[16]

Robinson pointed out that Kashmir had forged a language that aligned its struggle with the fight for human rights—and therefore, it was a matter of pride if the young sacrificed themselves in pursuit of the ideal. They were 'shahids'.

Traditionally, battlefield martyrs are viewed as shahid and pure, and during burial rites their bodies do not need to undergo the ritual of a purifying bath; they are laid to rest in bloodstained clothes as a sign of their martyrdom. But in the

---

[16]Cabeiri deBergh Robinson, *Body of a Victim, Body of Warrior: Refugee Families and the Making of Kashmiri Jihadists* (Oakland: University of California Press, 2013).

context of the Kashmir struggle, shahid comes with another connotation; civilians and even children who get killed in the course of the struggle are viewed as martyrs, even though they may not have been fighters, because they have borne 'witness to a start of violence or the dissolution of a state of justice [...] It is the dead body itself that testifies to the state of improper order by which such a death occurred.'[17]

Funerals are considered private affairs, but in the case of martyrs, they become public and political—so much so that the procession of the JKLF militant commander Ashfaq Majeed is still remembered as one of the largest gatherings. More recently, an estimated two lakh attended Burhan Wani's funeral, and funeral prayers were said at least fifteen times.

Women play a prominent role at such funerals, chanting and composing special songs of praise (*wahnuwan*) and recalling the sacrifices of their 'shahids', while scattering almonds and rose petals on the body.

Over the years, there have been some voices of dissent, questioning whether such sacrifice has yielded anything at all. The cynicism is countered with the argument that justice takes precedence over all things; that the fight against zulm is an end in itself, irrespective of whether the gains are tangible.

Misra herself, notwithstanding her dignified, matter-of-fact and even stately narration of events, continues to suffer. Her other son Sonu is a labourer and she and the family live in deprivation. All she has are tender memories of a lost son.

◆

Whilst Kashmiri women willingly threw themselves into the struggle for azadi, there were other entries into public

---

[17]Ibid.

spaces that were not voluntary. Kashmiri anthropologist Ather Zia has spoken of such forced decisions. The 'segue from domesticity into public [life]', she said was imposed when men began to get picked up increasingly by security troops supposedly for interrogation and were never seen again. Women, who earlier did not venture into a butcher's shop because it was a male-dominated space, were now forced to go to police stations, army camps, jails and courts in the state and outside in search of their missing sons and husbands. (To date, it is the women of the family—sisters, wives and daughters—who take on the challenge of inquring about the whereabouts of the male members of their family picked up under the PSA.)

This forced entry into public spaces was a double-edged sword. On the one hand, it became empowering—as in the case of Parveeena Ahangar and other members of the Association of Parents of Disappeared Persons who got together to spur political mobilization. On the other hand, the urgent need to establish contact with army camps and security personnel for crucial information left these women in a vulnerable position, open to cruel exploitation.

Zahir ud Din narrated an incident to illustrate how women were being forced to act as informers. He remembered how a teacher from Baramulla told him that once when he had gone to an army camp to meet a major, he happened to see a woman in burqa there. The major had refused to meet him, the reason being, as the teacher learnt years later, was that the army did not want anyone to know of its connection with the woman—she had been deployed as an informer from Sopore. 'It's said that she was subsequently killed by the security troops.' However, it is just as likely that she was killed by the militants for her links with the security forces.[18]

The scenario of unaccountability was made more complex by the presence of Ikhwanis. I got an inkling of this murky, shadowy world in which women fell at the hands of 'unknown armed men' when, in 2014, along with some friends, I visited a small village in Lolab, north Kashmir, where until recently, two major Rashtriya Rifles camps were positioned close by. In his house, we met Mohammed Yusuf, who opened an almirah and frantically looked for a polythene bag for a document he wanted to show us in connection with his sister's murder by two unidentified gunmen in 2002.

The men, he said, had appeared at the door, speaking in Urdu, demanding her whereabouts. Then, when she appeared, they shot her. The FIR that Yusuf finally recovered informed us that her death was by 'a firearm.'

The FIR did not furnish any more information. Who were the men? Were they militants? Or Ikhwanis unleashed by the Indian Army? Was the sister suspected of being an informer? Or did she have links with militants from the 1990s? Yusuf could not, or perhaps, dared not tell us more.

In 2003, the Jammu and Kashmir Coalition of Civil Society (JKCCS) decided to undertake a door-to-door first-of-its-kind survey—tellingly named 'Dead But Not Forgotten'—of an

---

[18]Similar stories about Kashmir's women have been documented by multiple books, theses and newspapers. Consider, for instance, Shodhganga—a portal hosted by the Information and Library Network (INFLIBNET) and promoted by the University Grants Commission (UGC)—which states, 'During the 1990s when the militancy was on [sic] peak, militants and Armed Forces were both using women as informers. [...] Two girls from Budgam, named Zaheeda and Nuzhat were shot at. First, the girls were dubbed as militant aides and then forced by the security personnel to work for them and when they refused, they were shot dead.' See <http://shodhganga.inflibnet.ac.in:8080/jspui/bitstream/10603/28683/12/12_chapter%203.pdf>, accessed on 27 May 2016.

entire district to find out who had been killed, where, when, how, and if possible, why. The aim was not only to arrive at such mathematical facts as the district's sex ratio, the numbers tortured or killed, migration statistics, and the sum total of temples and mosques razed, but also to come to grips with the true nature of the Kashmir conflict.

Khurram Parvez, a human rights activist from the JKCCS, informed me that what remained problematic was that fear still reigned supreme and many killings were not owned—no one seemed to come forward to take responsibility. Besides, many civilians changed dwellings to remain secure—indeed, this pattern of uprootings made it especially difficult to access and document narratives of violence in the Valley. But most importantly, the formal judicial order was seldom called upon to intervene—there was a 'trust deficit'.

This is the agony of Kashmir. A land where so many deaths will remain unknown, unknowable.

Chapter Three

WHO KILLED MY SON
The Wounded Spectators of the 1990s

It was Shazia Yousuf—a journalist and a professor in media studies at the Islamic University, Awantipora, pursuing a Panos fellowship on war and women—who opened my eyes to the nuanced ways in which militarization had impacted everyday life and larger events like birth and death. She recounted how her mother had been advised, because of certain complications, to go to the hospital for the delivery.

But on the day Shazia was to be born, a curfew had been imposed and the movement of vehicles restricted. Even as the women of the neighbourhood began discussing how they would get a pregnant woman to the hospital—what they should tell the soldiers—Shazia's mother protested. Raised in a conservative household, she could not tolerate the idea of unknown soldiers peering at her belly or commenting on her cries of pain. She refused to go. Much to everyone's dismay, she gave birth to her daughter at home. Shazia, in an essay titled 'The Hidden Damage' movingly captured this moment:

In the end, I was born in my childhood home, without

any medical assistance, in the same room where my elder siblings were born. 'I have no good memories of your birth,' my mother tells me. 'It only reminds me of the horrors.'[19]

The horrors of curfews and crackdowns were, not just disrupting the routine lives of Kashmiri women, but also violating their norms of sensitivity and dignity especially in a traditional milieu where it was taboo to speak of bodies and feelings, menstruation and sex.

Shazia has written powerfully about this invasion of privacy when troops ransacked private spaces so that 'cupboards and chests would lie open like fresh wounds, bleeding secrets of the family.' Her aunt, used to cringe when troops would deliberately scatter 'intimate objects' like sanitary pads, tweezers and cosmetics. Once a village elder was called by the soldiers to read aloud the stashed-away love letters of a young girl.

◆

Even as private selves were being made public, violence was being perpetrated at many levels. Homes were razed, families were torn apart and horrific massacres of entire neighbourhoods took place. For women, the scars ran deep.

In remote areas like Lolab, the plight of women was particularly precarious. Roshan Jan told me how troops would keep barging into her home even after her husband was picked up and presumably killed. One day, her home and belongings were burnt to ashes and she was compelled

---

[19]'Hidden Damage', *Guernica*, in <https://www.guernicamag.com/daily/shazia-yousuf-the-hidden-damage/>, 2 October 2014, accessed on 3 June 2016.

to flee to Srinagar—where she lived for many years.

In the multi-layered conflict, other women and children were caught up in the savagery unleashed by Special Police Officers (SPOs) and the army on families connected to militants. Many of them were almost acts of personal vendetta like the Salian massacre of 1998—in which nineteen people, including eleven children and five women (one pregnant), were shot dead[20] followed by a massacre in Mohra Bachai less than a year later.

On the morning of 3 August 2015, I witnessed the frail figure of Zahida—the sole survivor of the Mohra Bachai massacre—summoning up every bit of courage to join a few men in a silent protest near Press Colony. Zahida, in her statement, which has been recorded before the International People's Tribunal on Human Rights and Justice in Kashmir (IPTR), recounted the blood-soaked events of 29 June 1999, in which fifteen members of a joint family, including six children, were massacred at night in Mohra Bachai, a village in the Poonch district of Jammu. The alleged perpetrators include SPOs, personnel of the Indian Army and a deputy superintendent of police who is still holding a high post.[21]

While Zahida (and her unborn baby) miraculously got away, she lost her young husband Nissar and most of her in-laws. She is still haunted by what she saw that night—the

---

[20]'The survivors, who are also witnesses of the case, said their family members was [sic] eliminated by four special police officers (SPOs) and personnel from the Army.' In Naseer Ganai, 'CBI Slammed by Survivors for "Inaction" over Salian Massacre', Daily Mail, in <http://www.dailymail. co.uk/indiahome/article-2715018/CBI-slammed-survivors-inaction-Salian-massacre.html#ixzz4AEHSM4Mh>, accessed on 31 May 2016.
[21]'Families of Salian, Mohra Bachai Massacres Protest in Kashmir', Kashmir Times, in <http://www.kashmirtimes.in/newsdet.aspx?q=43609>, 3 August 2015, accessed on 1 June 2016.

way the gunmen tried to raze the house and, in doing so, dispose of the bodies of the dead.

◆

Then there were 'half-widows'—a curious word that became a part of Kashmir's lexicon during the nineties, and that persists till date—to describe women whose husbands have gone missing or have suffered enforced disappearance. These are women compelled by circumstances to live not just in emotional limbo—forever uncertain if their spouse is alive or dead, if he has been detained or if his remains have been hastily buried in an anonymous graveyard—but also under precarious socio-economic conditions.

In the 1990s, men were the chief bread earners in Kashmir—so the disappearance of a husband made a wife dependent on her in-laws or her maternal home. Moreover, since the husbands of half-widows were not officially declared dead, there remained a great deal of confusion over inheritance, property rights and bank transfers, all of which require death certificates.

Under such circumstances, to make ends meet, many half-widows were forced to seek employment, but since the majority lacked education or vocational skills, they remained unskilled labourers. To supplement their meagre income and run the household, their children would be forced to drop out of school and work in the carpet-making or affiliated industries.

Economic problems were only compounded by social isolation. It was not uncommon for the in-laws to blame the hapless wife, term her as unlucky, refuse shelter to her and her children, or offer a home only to their male grandchildren.

It also was not uncommon for a half-widow to subsist

under a cloud of suspicion—she was now a single woman—and for society to exert control over her movements, or for her in-laws to force her to remarry within the family—a tradition that found wide social acceptance.

The subject of remarriage was in itself fraught with uncertainty, with clerics disagreeing on the number of years a half-widow has to wait before remarrying. At one point, it was seven years but, in 2014, some clerics decreed that remarriage was permissible after four years. Today, there are half-widows who say they rejected the idea of remarriage because they do not believe their children, especially their daughters, will be wholly accepted by a new husband, or because they fear that matrimony will get in the way of their full-time struggle for justice.

Not surprisingly, many half-widows carried severe psychological wounds. Sabia who works with the Association of Parents of Disappeared Persons (APDP) spoke to me of medical problems half-widows confronted, especially in remote districts. Practically imprisoned within the four walls of their home, they were known to suffer from depression, anxiety and post-traumatic stress disorders. When they needed psychiatric help, such intervention was riddled with societal stigma—which meant that few women sought mental health care. Another social worker spoke about how there was social friction at home after a distraught woman took sedatives that had been prescribed to her. So, there would be complaints that she was sleeping too much, not making breakfast for the children, and neglecting her maternal and familial duties.

During one of my many visits to Kashmir, I accompanied an internee with APDP to the house of a half-widow. She revealed how helpless she felt in the early years after her husband went missing. Her parents wanted her to remarry but she resisted because she had children, one of them a girl, and most men would demand that she abandon her daughter.

Another half-widow M (name withheld on request), who was living with her in-laws, told me that she had been two months pregnant in 1997 when her husband had been picked up; he never returned. She scoured every police station she knew after the birth of her daughter. Someone told her that her husband was alive in Udhampur jail, but was offered little else by way of information. Finally, she pleaded with the jail staff to pass on a message to her husband, wherever he happened to be—that he was now a father of a baby girl. She is not sure if he ever got the message.

At this point the sister-in-law interrupted. All the family sought was a simple answer—was the man alive or dead? She said that the household had paid lakhs to *mukhbirs* (informers) for news, but it was all in vain. Her comment underlined a dubious industry that had erupted to exploit the phenomenon of men disappearing—a coterie of 'messengers' who made thousands of rupees by purportedly carrying missives for those who had vanished. In cahoots with them were fortune tellers and 'holy men', who preyed on the people who lived in doubt.

Even while agonizing over a question that could never be fully resolved, M found strength in her own way. She told me furtively—and begged me not to relay it to her sister-in-law—that she now had a cellphone with which she could network with other half-widows. She added that she believed she had only one true relative in the world—'Jiji' or Parveena Ahanger who heads the Association of Parents of Disappeared Persons, an organization that had been instrumental in securing an education for her daughter.

M's resilience is commendable. There are others who have found themselves getting pulled into a vortex of grief and penury, from which they cannot emerge. Even the ex gratia relief that has been extended by the J&K government seven years after a spouse goes missing can create a wedge between half-widows and their in-laws.

For, according to the Muslim personal law, a wife is entitled to only one-eighth of the amount and the rest is given to the deceased's parents. Besides, many parents and half-widows disagree over whether state-sponsored relief ought to be accepted. By taking such money, can they rescue their household from destitution, or are they, in fact, dishonouring the memories of those potentially dead?

◆

This brings one to a very important question. How Kashmiri men and women view government aid and ex gratia relief. The answer is layered. There are times when they choose to accept relief but declare that it cannot be seen as a compromise—that their fight for justice will go on, which is a stance adopted by Zaheeda, survivor of the Mohra Bachai massacre.

There are other occasions when relief has been welcomed—when the amount of compensation offered is seen as an acknowledgment of the heinousness of the crime committed. In 2011, Judge F.M. Ibrahim Kalifulla, in his verdict on the enforced disappearance of young Mushtaq Ahmad Dar—who had been picked up by the 20 Grenadiers of the Indian Army in April 1997—ruled for a compensation of ₹10 lakh to be awarded to the family. He noted that it was a crime of such grave magnitude that it shocked the conscience of the court.[22]

---

[22]Ishfaq Tantry, *HC's Landmark Judgement*, in <http://www.jammu-kashmir.

Then there is the story of Mehbooba, survivor of the Mashali Mohalla carnage, who was the first woman in the state to have been given ex gratia payment. Shazia Yusuf, who documented Mehbooba's story[23] told me how it marked the beginning of her own career as a journalist with a gender perspective. Shazia thought Mehbooba's story would be a routine one but realized it was much more. At one level, it was a poignant tale of a woman, who watched three members of her family get killed on 6 August 1990, when a battalion of the Border Security Force (BSF), under the garb of conducting a search operation, brutally attacked civilians in their homes in Mashali Mohalla, Srinagar. On the other, it is also about ways in which a patriarchal society could inflict grievous wounds and cause enormous hidden damage to the psyche of a woman and her children.

Mehbooba recalled the night, before the catastrophe, when she had been preparing dinner for her husband Bashir Ahmed Baig and two children—six-year-old Aijaz and seventeen-year-old Muzaffar. Two children, Nazima and Muneer were spending the night at their uncle's home in the neighbourhood. While Mehbooba was tenderly feeding chicken to a sickly Aijaz, coaxing him to eat, she heard loud noises, gunfire, shouts, and the shattering of window panes. Even as Mehbooba tried shielding her trembling children, the door burst open and security personnel stormed in. Some tried to disrobe her, and as she closed her eyes, she heard a volley of gunfire. Abruptly, the men let her go. When Mehbooba

---

com/archives/archives2011/kashmir20110402c.html>, accessed on 3 June 2016.
[23]Shazia Yousuf, 'After the Dark Night', *Kashmir Reader*, in <http://www.kashmirlife.net/after-the-dark-night-660/>, 22 July 2010, accessed on 25 July 2016.

opened her eyes, she found her family lying in a pool of blood.

Hurriedly she approached her husband who was barely conscious and told him that she had escaped a rape bid. She spotted Muzaffar but his body was pock-marked with wounds. Aijaz lay with a bullet in his chest, his mouth open with, partially chewed food dribbling out. Mehbooba quickly wiped away those morsels, hoping to hear gasps of breath. When she did, she yelled for help. One soldier came back—not to help—but to shoot her in the shoulder. Mehbooba crumpled, her family dead or dying around her.

Through the night (and many nights after) she wondered: Was her husband comforted when she conveyed to him that she had not been raped? Did her young son get any sustenance at all from the few morsels of food she had put into his mouth?

It was only the next morning that Mehbooba was found and hospitalized—her two sons and husband were dead. When former Divisional Commissioner Wajahat Habibullah met her in the hospital and proposed monetary compensation, Mehbooba's first instinct was to refuse the offer—and she did. But then, she faced a series of difficulties—her husband's family refused to grant her shelter saying that she now had no right over her husband's property. Also, her embroidery work was not enough to sustain her—so, finally, she approached Habibullah to ask for the compensation he had promised.

Shazia Yousuf notes that Mehbooba not only became the first person to receive ex gratia relief from the government but her case compelled the 'then divisional commissioner, Wajahat Habibullah, to devise a formal procedure of providing jobs and ex gratia relief to the families of victims.[24]'

Habibullah, in his book, *My Kashmir*, states:

---

[24]Ibid.

The prospect of restitution opened the door for people to approach the commissioner's office for relief, [and] the relief process became a tenuous thread that linked the government and the general public. Does Mehbooba know that she initiated the first hesitant step towards the restoration of peace in Kashmir?[25]

Shazia's report quotes Habibullah but also weaves in Mehbooba's counter-narrative. 'I didn't want to rebuild my life with the money of a country whose people killed my family. But then everyone told me, it is the money of our state and not theirs.'[26]

◆

Then, there are grief-stricken Kashmiri women who have refused to touch a rupee of the compensation offered, denouncing it as 'blood money'. It was in Shopian that I met Kulsum and her husband Nazir Ahmed—a retired employee of the Jammu and Kashmir fire service department, who had been honoured by the state for saving lives during the attack on the Kashmir Assembly in 2001[27]. The honour notwithstanding, the conflict ruthlessly engulfed the family. Kulsum and Nazir lost all their three sons.

I was graciously welcomed into their home in Shopian where, despite being busy with last-minute preparations for a Hajj pilgrimage, Nazir and Kulsum made time to speak to me at length. Their saga of grief began on 3 March 2003, when

---

[25]Ibid. Quoted from Wajahat Habibullah, *My Kashmir: The Dying of the Light* (New Delhi: Penguin, 2011).
[26]Shazia Yousuf, 'After the Dark Night', *Kashmir Reader*, in <http://www.kashmirlife.net/after-the-dark-night-660/>, 22 July 2010, accessed on 25 July 2016.
[27]See also the author's essay 'No Place for Picnics', *Himal*, 4 April 2013.

the second of three sons—the spiritually inclined Naseer (or Gashe as he was affectionately called)—left their house after lunch to offer prayers at the mosque. He failed to return home. His disappearance sparked speculation, with some suggesting that he had joined the militants, and others like Kulsum claiming that he became a victim of custodial violence after being picked up by security troops for interrogation. What was clear was that Gashe became one more statistic in Kashmir's long list of the 'missing'.

Eventually, Kulsum got news about Gashe when her eldest son, Nevli Hilal, aged nineteen, received a phone call from an unknown person informing him that his missing brother had been shot dead by an army official. Nevli collapsed on hearing the news and suffered a heart attack. He was declared dead when brought in at the hospital.

Five years later—according to Kulsum—the youngest and only surviving son, Sajjad, aged seventeen, who had been making his way back home after offering prayers at his elder brother's grave, was shot dead by the much feared Special Operations Group near Jamia Masjid. It was a Friday, the town was tense because of the ongoing Amarnath land row, and Sajjad, who happened to have rushed to douse a fire near the mosque, got targeted, and died before he could get assistance.

While Kulsum and her husband kept asserting that the use of firearms on protesters and bystanders was totally unjustified since no curfew had been declared, officials from the CID (Criminal Investigation Department) presented a new set of facts—they accused Sajjad of being a stone-pelter and added that he had died a week later. The couple vehemently denied this and Kulsum's husband approached the Shopian SHO. Here, he was informed that an FIR had been filed not only against his dead son but also against him for trying to attack a police station.

Two years later, Kulsum and Nazir were told that the state was granting them 1 lakh rupees as ex gratia relief for the death of their youngest son. Both categorically refused to accept the sum and gave a statement to the effect before the magistrate's team. Nazir and Kulsum said, 'I told them not to rub salt on our wounds with the offer. What would we do with the money? We would rather beg than accept this.'

As I left Kulsum's home, she told me that in her twilight years she wanted nothing but justice for her youngest son, and the truth behind her second son's disappearance. Her friends informed me that Kulsum still clung to the hope that somehow Gashe was alive, and that, one day, he would walk in through the doorway.

◆

Sometimes it is not just the militant but his family that has to pay the price of rebellion with relentless oppression on family members continuing even decades after he has been killed. I came upon one such story in the picturesque village of Laroo in Kulgam district. There, I saw two stately houses built with the small bricks that are peculiar to the Valley. I was informed that there used to be *three* such houses—the first 'pucca' constructions in the village. In one such house lived Zareena, her husband Mohammed Ayub Ganaie and their extended family—until the house was razed to the ground. The inhabitants had fled to the fields and escaped when troops entered the village.

I was now led into a more humble home inhabited by the Ganaie family, and was swept into an enormous bear hug by Zareena. After the customary round of formalities, she began narrating her story in fragmented anguished outbursts, with her husband, daughter Shaukya and daughter-in-law occasionally intervening. A young boy, her grandson, sat quietly in a corner.

In 1991, said Zareena, one of her sons, Khursheed Ahmed Lone, joined the thousands of youngsters crossing the border. Three years later, he returned as a militant and would make quiet visits to his family home. He also began imparting the teachings of the Koran to villagers, said Zareena. Khursheed was also perhaps involved in a recruitment drive and by 1996, at least half the population in the area was linked to the militancy.

There was a camp of the Rashtriya Rifles close to the village that must have got wind of Khursheed's activities. The reprisals were swift and Khursheed was killed in an encounter.

Yet, even after his death, Zareena claimed, persistent attempts were made to intimidate the family. On one occasion, Khursheed's father and younger brother Riyaz were picked up from the fields for interrogation. 'The troops said they would keep them prisoners till we revealed Khursheed's whereabouts. But my son had already been killed. My husband was subjected to electric shocks, force fed water, beaten severely and burnt—his leg is permanently damaged.

'Soldiers would come to my house and smash all my pots and cooking utensils; one placed the butt end of his gun on my shoulder and abused me. Whenever we could, we'd run away and hide in the fields.

'At other times, we women watched, helpless. First, they took away my fifteen-year-old son—it was a day before Id— and his hands were tied behind his back. Then, they targeted Nazra Begum, a relative particularly fond of my Khursheed— by barging into her room at midnight just two days after she had delivered a child. They also prevented the wife of one of our sons from returning to us after she had delivered a child at her parents' home. She waited for two long years to come back to her husband. Finally, our house...'

The destruction of the house spelt economic ruin. It also spelt the demise of a social support system. The neighbours, fearing the wrath of the state, stopped associating with the Ganaie family and the village sarpanch refused to issue identity papers. Since no Kashmiri can step out without this vital document, the family cannot leave the hamlet and seek employment. They are forced to work as labourers. 'We remain faceless, identity-less,' said an anguished Zareena.

Chapter Four

DON'T THINK, MY CHILD
The Tehreek Generation

'Your generation brought in the tehreek,' the 1989-born writer, Uzma Falak, was often told by her mother.

Like so many of Kashmir's children who grew familiar with words like 'curfew', 'crackdown' and 'tehreek', the conflict coloured Uzma's life—so much so that almost every childhood event came to be bookmarked by the larger struggle for azadi. 'People would say, "I remember you were so-many-years-old when a 'particular person' in the resistance was picked up".'

Gunshots and cordons seemed light years away as Uzma and I sat in Naseem Bagh in Kashmir University on a beautiful spring afternoon. Uzma is a woman with many identities—a gold medallist in mass communications from Jamia Millia Islamia, a keen art and poetry enthusiast, an author and filmmaker. But that day, she was a child of the conflict, as she attempted to sift through overlapping memories, and describe the summer of 1996.

'I remember it clearly,' she said, 'it is etched in my mind. I had gone out with my father to buy household supplies and was given a doll. As I clutched it in one hand and held onto my father with the other, we made our way back home which was in a volatile area of Srinagar. Just a short distance away from our house, we saw that the neighbourhood had been cordoned off. There was a crackdown. Troops had gathered on the streets and nobody was being allowed in.

'Our house was just a few metres away from us, so my father urged me to approach one of the army men. "Ask him," he said, "if he'll allow you to go home." I was scared. But I couldn't ignore my father's request as I was very close to him.

'I crossed the road. I was the only civilian to attempt that. I remember the army man I approached—his boots, his eyes, even his bandana—the dark strip that would cover the hair and part of the soldiers' faces when they were geared up for battle. For me, those were symbols that invoked fear. Nervously, I asked him if I could go home. My mother was at the window and she, too, pleaded with him with frantic gestures.

'He remained unmoved. He asked me to go back from where I had come. My father and I spent the night at a relative's home. I could not have understood the dynamics of occupation at that time. But, as a child, I understood that I was not allowed to go home.'

What followed was a childhood marked by anxiety. Panic and paranoia were palpable in the stories Uzma shared—be it when her brother's toy gun had to be quickly hidden from the ransacking troops; or when her mother misplaced a cupboard key and grew frantic with worry—what if the soldiers wanted *that* almirah opened? Or the terror when two army men were refused entry into a room where the Koran was kept—'My mother said that this was a sacred space. I was scared witless. I thought, "Why doesn't she just keep quiet? What if they shoot her?'"

Fear was a constant factor in the fragments of recollection, too. One night, a school-going Uzma stayed up late, past 2 a.m., engrossed in her water colours in the living room. Suddenly, she heard a knock on the main door. Her mother rushed out of the bedroom, visibly nervous, and urged her daughter to switch off the lights and leave the living room without making a sound. The next morning, the family learnt that the knock was that of a neighbour who had had returned home late after a wedding. Not all stories ended in an anti-climax.

Uzma's voice turned low. 'I meant to write about this episode I am narrating but haven't summoned up the nerve. One night, again, we heard someone loudly banging against something. We were alarmed. My father wondered aloud if we ought to investigate—but no one dared step out. It was madness to venture out into the streets after 6 p.m. I tried to peer through the windows to see if we could make sense of what was happening. But it was pitch dark, nothing was visible.'

She continued, 'In the morning, the neighbourhood learnt that a poor, mentally-challenged man who used to live in a small tin-shed outside our home, had collected scraps of paper for a bonfire, possibly to keep himself warm and had accidently immolated himself. He had been calling for help; that is what accounted for the banging. His charred remains were found.'

For a young Uzma, there were no safe spaces. Not at home. Not in the streets. This was reiterated when her school in Lal Chowk—the emotional heart of Kashmir, named after Moscow's Red Square—witnessed a huge bomb blast close to its gates. 'I was tying my headscarf before I stepped out and that is what saved me. After the blast, everyone was alarmed. I tried desperately to find my brother. I pushed my way through the crowds, rushed past my classmates prone on the road, some blood-stained, some crying. I heard a visually-challenged teacher ask repeatedly, 'What's happening?' I had no answers.

'Finally, I called home, and was told that my brother was safe. So I too found my way back to my residence. Everywhere, there were troops frisking school bags. "What's this?" I was asked. "Lunch box," I snapped back, my anger obvious. A part of me was pleased that I had confronted the security troops in my own way. I thought my mother would commend me for my bravery.

'But no. Instead, my mother scolded, "You should never have done that!" I was traumatized.'

Uzma, also recalled, 'When I was very little, I would sometimes try to hide within the folds of my grandmother's cloak to escape the gaze of the troops. As a teenager, I took to sitting in cupboards. Enclosed spaces actually made me feel safe—as though I was back in the womb—in that buffer between the worlds of life and death.'

◆

A whole generation of Kashmir's children grew up knowing a world contained within four walls. Uzma told me, 'We couldn't move out. Most of my childhood pictures are set within my residence. *School se ghar, ghar se school.* (School to home, home to school.) That was the routine.'

Malik Sajad, a promising cartoonist, depicts this in one of his early drawings—a house door, slightly ajar, and the hand of young boy stretching out into the world, reaching for a cricket ball nestled between the boots of a soldier. Elsewhere, he depicts a band of brothers playing indoor cricket, and calculating runs by flipping the pages of a book.[28]

Designer and researcher Mahum Shabir, too, learnt to find diversions in her house. Her mother, who was a doctor, took up gardening with a passion and Mahum was given a little studio of her own—a small garage—where she had access to moulding clay and canvasses, and could sculpt and paint. Mahum said, 'My parents were constantly worried because of the presence of army personnel outside our home—so if I ventured out, it was only with my parents—and then, we'd go to the Dal Lake. Otherwise, I was at home most of the time with art tools for company.'

For Uzma Falak, dolls were her childhood friends. 'I played with them, I had nobody else. On Id, when we had a holiday, my mother would wait by the gate with a bowl of dry fruits and offer it to any girl going past, hoping she would come in and play with me.'

There were times, though, when even homes became inaccessible. Uzma recalled how troops would march in and sit in front of her family's television, back when the Mahabharata was being telecast. 'They would be glued to the TV set, and my mother would have to make tea for them. The rest of us would wait in the verandah, wondering when we would be able to reclaim the drawing room.'

Then there were days when the the streets would become places where women would gather to be together during the dreaded crackdowns. 'So many lovely dinners were abandoned as my mother would exclaim, "*Wathev, bei chu tchalun chu!* (Come on, we have to run away yet again!)", and we would leave our home.'

---

[28]Malik Sajad, *Munnu: A Boy from Kashmir* (New Delhi: HarperCollins, 2015).

Shazia Yousuf, also a child of the tehreek, recalls how children became witnesses to death and loss. 'The enormity of this became clear the day my sister and I visited our childhood home. Looking down the street, we said, "That's the house of so-and-so who died. That house, further down the street, is the home where *he* lived before he was killed." Really... eight boys known to us were dead.'

Violence was rubbing off onto a whole generation's speech and thoughts. Shazia remembered: 'One day, when I was about five years old, my sister and I happened to run across the road to buy ice cream and I got hit by a scooter. A young boy of our neighbourhood, Javed, came to my rescue and took me to a clinic. By then, there was blood everywhere and I was hysterical. I started screaming, hurling all the curses I had heard women utter: "May you be killed! May you die! May soldiers take you away!" Imagine that. A five year old picking up such language and insults!'

In a tragic twist, eighteen-year-old Javed died within a year. Shazia's sister told her that it was because of her expletives. 'For years I was filled with dread and guilt. I really thought my profanities had killed him.'

But the most poignant loss of all was that of Mogli.

'There was a trader in our neighbourhood,' Shazia informed me, 'who was always out travelling. One day, he brought back with him an injured monkey. All of us persuaded him to keep Mogli as a pet. Soon, it became our beloved companion. One night, there were gunshots. Mogli died. We learnt that the troops in the bunker had shot the monkey, mistaking its shadow for something menacing. We were inconsolable. We laid Mogli in a coffin and took her around, shouting slogans, mimicking the many funeral processions we had seen. We yelled, "Mogli was innocent. Why did you kill her?"

'The troops were actually shaken by the incident. For them, Mogli was Hanuman, (the monkey god revered by Hindus). For us, she was a friend. And she had been killed.'

Mahum Shabir too recalls a very early memory about the death of a relative—a cousin—who had been shot and whose body had been found under gruesome circumstances. Mahum saw people crying, she sensed the deep anguish of those around her, and while she didn't gather all the details surrounding the violent death of her cousin, she gleaned that the 'situation outside' was in some way linked to his departure.

It is, perhaps, in light of this that a student of media studies, Afshan, told me, 'My mother's generation believed that death was foreshadowed by a red line in the sky. My generation has seen so much death that the sky should carry permanent red daubs.'

◆

Shazia's own recollections of trauma and her focus on how children were deeply affected by violence is reflected in her report on Mehbooba, the woman who was given ex gratia payment after three members of her family had been killed by the BSF. Mehbooba revealed to Shazia that Muneer, who had survived, because he was not at home that day, had begun avoiding his mother after the grisly incident and she couldn't understand why.

Much later, she learnt that this young boy had seen his mother being brought out of the room, her hair loose, her hands and clothes smeared with blood. Too little to know what had happened, he imagined that his mother had killed his father and brothers. In the absence of psychiatric care or emotional counselling, he nursed a misplaced anger and shock for years.

It was only when he grew up, and gathered the details of the night of 6 August 1990, that he realized how grievously he had misinterpreted the truth. 'I made my mother go through hell when she needed me the most,' he confided in journalist Shazia Yousuf, who interviewed him.[29]

As a child of the conflict, Muneer could not bring himself to complete his education; and as a mortified adult, could not pursue a fulfilling vocation. Muneer was the 'collateral damage' of the 1990s.

◆

How does one, in fact, gauge the extent of trauma that Kashmir's children suffered because of what they had seen and experienced? When I had visited Zareena's family in Kulgam, I had noticed how her young grandson sat quietly in a corner and appeared withdrawn. Shaukya, Zareena's unmarried daughter, revealed the reason for this behaviour. 'Once, security troops came into the village and were trying to attack the women. I managed to run away, although someone did try to grab me. My little nephew, who was still crawling at that time, must have seen *something* that night—maybe the way the attackers were pouncing on the women. From that day on, his speech has been affected and he can barely string a few sentences together.'

In the total absence of psychiatric care or emotional counselling it is impossible to diagnose his impairment or measure his traumatized state.

---

[29]Shazia Yousuf, 'After the Dark Night', *Kashmir Reader*, in <http://www.kashmirlife.net/after-the-dark-night-660/>, 22 July 2010, accessed on 25 July 2016.

Shaukya added how children were made to play as informers during the militancy. 'Soldiers would hand out ten-rupee notes in exchange for information,' she said.

◆

Then, there are the Valley's children held under the notorious Public Safety Act and people fighting for their release. It was in the *Amnesty* report, 'A "Lawless" Law' that I first read about Mushtaq Ahmad Sheikh, born in the 1990s:

> Fourteen-year-old Mushtaq Ahmad Sheikh was held in administrative detention for nearly ten months from 21 April 2010 to 10 February 2011. He was arrested on 9 April 2010 in a criminal case of rioting and attempt to murder, allegedly as part of a stone-pelting mob. Released on bail eight days later, he was detained under the PSA on 21 April. The grounds of detention state his age to be nineteen although his family told Amnesty International that he was born in 1996 and is only fourteen years old.[30]

I managed to visit Mushtaq's family of seven sisters in downtown Srinagar with the help of Uzma Falak, who had interviewed the members of this household earlier. I had been told that the family was poverty-stricken, but I was not prepared for what I saw—an entrance to a dwelling that lay in complete darkness. I had to feel my way up a steep flight of steps, cut into mud and stone, to reach a narrow room— this was their home, scarcely bigger than a little verandah. Within, personal belongings had been stashed away in plastic

---

[30]'A "Lawless" Law"', *Amnesty*, in <http://www.amnestyusa.org/sites/default/files/asa200012011en_11.pdf>, accessed on 8 July 2016.

bags—rows of them that hung from the ceiling.

I was told that Mushtaq, a student of class eight and the only son of his family, had been arrested, along with several young boys in Nowhatta, under the PSA. In the days to come, Mushtaq would be ferried across across many jails, including Kot Bhalwal in Jammu.

Mushtaq's father, a labourer who been caught in a cross-firing and had suffered a bullet injury on his shoulder, was infirm and earned a tiny stipend doing odd jobs at a mosque. So, Mushtaq's mother, who had little or no experience with long journeys, took it upon herself to catch buses—accompanied by one or two of her daughters—and visit her son, wherever he happened be—oftentimes going hungry for the duration of the trip. Sometimes, these trips were in vain for the authorities would have given them incorrect information about Mushtaq's whereabouts.

I learnt from journalist, Dilnaz Boga, that Mushtaq's sisters, when not accompanying their mother across jails, used to protest for their brother's freedom in 2010—raising slogans and creating quite a stir in the Sunday market near Polo View. Of the sisters, it was Sakina who was the 'ring leader', the strategist. Dressed in a pair of jeans and a faux leather jacket, and sporting short hair, she had a distinctive presence. Sakina told me she had to abandon school so that she could take up the cause of her brother and protest at Nowhatta Chowk, outside the police station, or at the Press Colony near Lal Chowk.

Sakina also informed me that currently her brother was out on bail. But with multiple cases against him, he had little freedom—he was still a youth being pursued—and had to routinely leave home. 'There are times,' she revealed, 'when policemen come late at night, even at 2 a.m., and stand below our family's room, demanding to know the whereabouts of our brother.'

It is believed that the family and boy are being targeted because he has refused to turn informer.

If Mushtaq's childhood has been frittered away, Sakina's is one of rebellion. She dresses like a young lad and says that from an early age she had liked to dress in Khan suits. On the streets, she strides around and is assertive—wolf-whistling to summon a passing autorickshaw—and, often even referring to herself in the male gender. Is she defying enculturation? Has assuming responsibility at a young age had a liberating effect or is it a way of asserting identity in a family of seven sisters? Are there issues of sexuality? Her father had told me they have no objection to the way she dresses and that it is a personal choice.

There are no neat answers but Sakina demonstrates how, in a troubled land, she has been able to tackle forces of oppression by the state *and* shake off the shackles of society. She lives in a small room but it has expanded into a huge space of personal liberty.

◆

Among the most wounded in spirit of Kashmir's children are those whose fathers suffered enforced disappearances, whose mothers are half-widows. According to Zahoor Wani, formerly with the Association of Parents of Disappeared Persons, these children are often psychologically fragile. They have been witness to a mother's grief and a father's sudden disappearance, have been compelled to lead isolated lives and often feel stigmatized, especially on occasions like 'parents' day' at school.

Author Zahir ud Din, who was part of the team for *Buried*

Evidence (brought out by the International People's Tribunal on Human Rights and Justice)[31] and who has written a book on the disappeared—*Did They Vanish in Thin Air?*[32]—described how the eldest offspring of half-widows were forced to grow up too soon and likened their emotional state to a balloon inflated beyond capacity.

He spoke about the daughter of a half-widow living in extreme penury along the banks of the Jhelum. The seven-year-old girl told Zahir ud Din that she wished that her mother would remarry. She felt burdened by her mother's huge worries and fears of the future. 'Some years later,' Zahir ud Din said, 'I learnt that the girl had taken to drugs.'

Half-widows, denied money and social support, were sometimes compelled to split up a family. Tahira, was one such woman that Shazia Yousuf spoke to. She said that, when her husband disappeared and she was left with three children she tried to make the best of the situation—taking her kids along with her while scouring military camps, jails and detention centres. But when her savings ran dry, she had no option but to place one son in Rahat Manzil, another in Miskeen Bagh, and the third in Baitul Hilal—all orphanages—so she could carry on with investigations and inquiries. When Tahira's children returned to stay with her, they were bitter and angry, unable to make sense of why their mother had abandoned them. One of her sons brusquely asked, 'Was I an orphan? If my father has died, why do you still search for him?'

Months later, Tahira had only this to tell Shazia: 'It is not death where you mourn and overcome grief. When a loved

---

[31]See *Buried Evidence*, in <http://www.kashmirprocess.org/reports/graves/>, accessed on1 July 2016.
[32]Zahir ud Din, *Did They Vanish in Thin Air?* (Jammu and Kashmir: Sabha Publications, 1995).

one [disappears], you don't want to mourn but hope for his comeback. [...] I feel it is my duty to trace him [...].'[33]

◆

The regrets and anguish of mothers for 'children without childhood' was echoed by Mubeena, a school teacher. She spoke of how agonized she was because her children, growing up in the nineties, were deprived of the simple joys that she had so enjoyed in her own childhood. She spoke of how once her son returned from a school picnic with his tiffin box still packed. 'He told me that none of the children were allowed to get off the bus at the picnic spot because it had grown dark and the school authorities were apprehensive about their safety.'

Mubeena recalled a night of terror when, during a furious gun-battle in the neighbourhood, she had to flee clutching her young daughter to her chest, even as gunshots reverberated around her. Even greater horrors had unfolded such as the beheading of the village carpenter, and Mubeena, as a mother, felt impelled to allay her children's fears during those dark days. This has been memorialized by her son Arif in a poem titled 'A Conversation with My Mother on One of the Last Days of Ramzan'. A few lines read:

...Don't think about the war, pleads my mother
her quivering voice a willow twig in August
and a mid-summer drizzle hanging in her eyes.
Don't think of the still-bleeding throat of the carpenter

[33]See Shazia Yousuf, 'The Lonely and Painful Life of Tahira', *Greater Kashmir*, in <http://www.greaterkashmir.com/news/gk-magazine/the-lonely-and-painful-life-of-tahira/183488.html>, 8 January 2015, accessed on 7 July 2016.

whose headless body left the first floor of our home
without doors and windows for twenty years...

...

Thoughts are very expensive, my dear.
Kashmiris cannot afford them.
So don't think, my child, don't think.

◆

Chapter Five

HOW DO I TELL MY STORY?
Sexual Violence in the Valley[34]

The road wound upwards, past torrential streams, meadows and pine trees. This was Gujjar country, home to semi-nomadic pastoral communities; their transient lifestyle meant that they remained along the peripheries of Kashmiri society. Labelled as among those most loyal to India in Kashmir—which, in turn, signified that they were viewed with much suspicion, especially during the 1990s—the dominant impression even today is that the Gujjars have been cultivated by intelligence agencies to act as informers regarding militant activities. But reality is far more complex. The conflict and occupation impacted their lifestyle and livelihood, and they were denied access to the higher meadows. They also had to bear the brunt of violence and the remote terrain meant their women were even more vulnerable to sexual violence.

I got to understand the anguish of Gujjar women during my visit to south Kashmir in May 2013, when my friends and I attempted to locate a young woman called Pakeeza

---

[34]The names of rape victims and their relatives have been changed in this chapter as per norms regarding reports on sexual violence.

(name changed) who, eleven years earlier, had allegedly been a victim of sexual violence. A little after Sonarshbrar, when we finally left our car and climbed up a bridle path, we found a small mud dwelling.

Here, I joined Pakeeza who had been summoned from the higher meadows where she had been looking after sheep and goats. We sat with another woman in an inner room while the men waited outside. In the late afternoon, shadows lengthened, and as we talked the sense of isolation was almost complete.

We learnt that it was, perhaps, on one such afternoon in 2004 that two army personnel barged into the then twenty-year-old's home near Bunishpura. In her narrative, Pakeeza was unable to recall the exact date of the incident. She could only confirm that it was the maize-harvesting season. This is indicative of how difficult it is to document incidents of violence within communities that record events not according to a western calendar, but by keeping track of nature's cycles.

Pakeeza told us that she had been making tea for two of her husband's relatives—believed to be militants—when they saw troops approaching and ran away. The security personnel, dragged Pakeeza to another room in full view of some members of her husband's family and allegedly sexually assaulted her. Pakeeza said she had no recollection of what ensued. In her words she 'lost consciousness'.

Soon after, a security cordon was enforced around the area, making it difficult for Pakeeza to venture out and record the crime. She recounted that a few days later, a senior army officer had offered the family a sum of ₹5,00,000 in exchange for silence; they were also assured that the perpetrators would be suspended.

This dangling of money was a cynical exercise in

manipulation whereby a poor family's sense of honour was commodified. It created marital discord. Pakeeza's husband was made to believe that the 'compensation' was paid to Pakeeza's father. He also told activists that it was this suspicion that drove him to divorce Pakeeza.

In her story, Pakeeza told us that her husband was promised a job if he divorced her. He, in turn, became angry because he was never given one because Pakeeza had fled to Srinagar.

Pakeeza initially wanted to pursue the case in court but the Station House Officer (SHO) asked her to produce witnesses. This wasn't possible as all of them belonged to her former husband's family. The rupture in familial ties and bitterness over the manner in which she had been divorced robbed her of the will to fight. She consented to marry another person from the Gujjar family who, she said, knew she had been raped. Her husband, she said, does not bring up the topic.

Pakeeza's layered narrative, brought out how rape, honour and compensation played out in patriarchal structures. On the one hand, there was the commodification of her own dignity when the family was made a compensatory offer, without any regard for their expectations of justice. Then there was Pakeeza's own understanding of rape, rooted in patriarchal notions, in the belief that she was, in some way, guilty—evident in the way she suddenly said, *'Galti thee kyun ki militants hamaare thay.'* ('We made a mistake, the militants were from our community.') While she did sense that rape was being used as a weapon of war, she was still to arrive at the realization that there was no justification for the crime—that the violation of her autonomy and integrity was not acceptable and is an internationally recognized crime.

We had met Pakeeza thanks to the intervention of a Gujjar

elder. Six months later, my friends and I took up his invitation of hospitality by camping in his field for the night. Surrounded by the bleating of goats, we heard the Gujjar elder speak with sagacity about his community's role in Kashmiri politics, and of how two of his young sons had joined the struggle for azadi and had been killed. He added that he regretted the fact that many Kashmiris viewed the Gujjars as outsiders and questioned their loyalty—if the Gujjars had, on occasion, liaised with the army, Kashmiris, too, had become informers and Ikhwanis.

The next morning, as we ambled down the meadow, the Gujjar elder asked me to join his wife for a cup of tea. Pakeeza and a few other women were with her. As I entered the house, I was told that the elder's wife wanted to share something with me. However, she kept deflecting my questions and speaking, in general terms, of the intimidation of the troops in the nineties. Finally, when I began leaving the room, she pulled me back and then, after ensuring that the other women were out of the room, pulled the pheran's sleeve off her shoulder.

This simple gesture was her narrative. She had been disrobed and raped.

I later learnt that she had recounted the event to me at her husband's behest. His encouragement that she 'speak out' reminded me that men sometimes take the lead in breaking silences.

◆

In 2012–13, I set out to record cases of sexual violence linked to the conflict in Kashmir. The women courageously agreed to share their stories with me, even though I was a complete stranger.

I had, at first, set out with a sound recorder but soon

realized that some of my interviewees felt more comfortable when it was switched off. I also realized that their stories would not flow in a neat, ordered manner, but with hesitation and pauses, as though, even in the telling, they were battling fears of stigma or reprisal, denial and reluctance.

I also noticed that they never alluded to the actual act of rape or violence but brought it up in a vague manner. Most of them (like Pakeeza) simply said that they had lost consciousness or blanked out. I tried to respect their reticence. I have come to see that accepting the sounds of silence is a way of acknowledging a woman's dignity and pain.

Occasionally, I was puzzled by the lacunae in the telling of stories and seemingly contradictory bits of information. But it was a human rights activist who helped me understand these gaps and how so many women were still trying to come to terms with their trauma. He said that once he had asked a victim to clarify an apparent inconsistency and she had responded with some bewilderment, 'So what should I have told you? How should I tell my story?' The innocence and poignancy of that question—what should a woman tell or not tell?—was a stark reminder of just how difficult it is for female survivors of sexual violence to recount their tales.

How does she recall the nitty-gritty details of the violence inflicted on her and revisit dark memories when it is only natural for the mind to blur such moments or shut them out? How many times is she expected to keep telling her story?

How does she grapple with, not only the violence of the act, but also the violence of a society that shames her, the victim?

How does she remain true to herself and her story, when sections of society have already stigmatized her—viewing her as 'ruined', or having brought the crime upon herself?

How does she elucidate the sexual details when she comes

from a society where such talk is considered inappropriate? How does she receive the acknowledgment she needs for the brutal violation of her rights when gender-based violence has been an integral part of armed conflict throughout history? Most pertinently, what expectations can she hold vis-à-vis justice when judicial institutions have often failed to offer witness protection and when laws like AFSPA provide a protective cover to offenders?

In Kashmir, as in Manipur and other parts of the northeast, where AFSPA is in force, security personnel cannot be prosecuted—not even for a crime as heinous as rape—without the sanction of the Central government. Although, policemen are not officially covered under AFSPA, a blanket of impunity envelopes them, too. *Alleged Perpetrators: Stories of Impunity in Jammu and Kashmir* is a comprehensive dossier brought out in 2012 that examines roughly 214 cases of human rights violations, including enforced disappearances, torture, custodial deaths and sexual violence, and the role of 500 'alleged perpetrators', largely from the Indian Army, Paramilitary and Police force. The document notes the overwhelming reluctance to investigate:

> [...] in the name of countering militant violence the Indian state authorizes security forces to carry out all kinds of operations, often without adherence to laws and norms. [There is an] overwhelming reluctance to genuinely investigate or prosecute the armed forces for human rights violations. There may be the occasional willingness to order compensatory relief, but not to bring the perpetrators to justice.[35]

---

[35]See *Alleged Perpetrators*, in <http://kashmirprocess.org/reports/alleged_ Perpetrators.pdf>, accessed on 9 June 2016.

In 2013, the J&K government actually announced a victim compensation chart for rape survivors, which classified rape victims under different categories, one of them being 'raped in police custody'. Fortunately, the emphasis on compensation rather than punitive action came to be swiftly condemned.[36]

◆

My friends said they had heard of some particularly gruesome series of incidents that had occurred in 1997 at a home in Reshpora, south Kashmir, and we set off to record the events one morning. When we stopped for directions and asked, 'Do you know the residence of Ghulam who went missing?' we got the chilling reply, 'You mean the one who was abducted and killed? In Kashmir, the 'missing never come home.'

With that, we were led to Ghulam's home and met his family, who shared with us an account of all that they had lost one wintry night. Speaking in Koshur (Kashmiri), Ghulam's daughter Amira (name changed) and her son Abdul, (name changed) now in his twenties, spoke of the night of 2–3 January 1997, when an army official of 5 Rashtriya Rifles, camped at Batpora, came with his retinue at around 8 p.m., demanding a meeting with Ghulam. The official alleged that Ghulam had been secretly meeting Amira's former husband—a Hizb-ul-Mujahideen militant who had deserted her and with whom she had tried to sever links by filing for a divorce.

'We asked the official to return in the morning but he refused,' said Amira, even as she recounted how, just three days prior to that night, she had gone to military officials at

---

[36]Bashaarat Masood, 'J&K Govt Offers Rs 2 Lakh for Rape, Rs 3 Lakh for Rape in Police Custody, *The Indian Express*, in <http://archive.indianexpress.com/news/j-k-govt-offers-rs-2-lakh-for-rape-rs-3-lakh-for-rape-in-police-custody/1156709>, 18 August 2013, accessed on 9 June 2016.

the Batpora camp and begged that they stop harassing the family. She claimed that she had even paid a sum of ₹30,000 in a bid to stop the intimidation.

Abdul added, 'On that night of 2 January, the troops first slapped my mother and then attacked my grandfather. His head hit the floor. Perhaps, he was already dead when they dragged him away.'

Next, the bulbs were smashed and in the cover of darkness the personnel jumped on the defenceless women and young children in the house. In her account, Amira claimed that she managed to run away and hide in one of the public bathing spaces and that the children sought shelter in the neighbour's house. However, her fourteen-year-old sister Aneesa (name changed) failed to escape and was sexually assaulted. Amira did not divulge the details—all she said was that about two hours later, she saw a soldier coming out of the house, carrying the young Aneesa in his arms, trying to cover her with clothes.

The following day, Amira requested the mukadam (village headman) to urge the army to return her father's body. But she was advised to run away. Undeterred, the family filed an FIR on 5 January.

In response, the police charge-sheeted the alleged perpetrators and then, following the tenets of AFSPA, sought sanction for their prosecution. The request was declined on the grounds that there was no prima facie evidence against the personnel of 5 Rashtriya Rifles; and besides, Amira was the wife of a 'dreadful Hizb-ul-Mujahideen militant'. It was alleged that she had been forced to file a false allegation against the supposed perpetrators by anti-national elements who wished to malign the image of the forces.

The *Alleged Perpetrators* report, which went on to dissect this case, commented that the argument proffered—that

Amira's husband was a militant—was grounded in neither law nor logic.[37]

The SHRC (State Human Rights Commission) ultimately recommended punishing the prime perpetrator, granting ex gratia relief of ₹5,00,000 to Amira, and employment for her son on compassionate grounds. But this compensation was for the abduction. No punitive action was taken for the grisly crimes of abduction and sexual violence. Documents suggest that perhaps no court martial took place.

Amira, in her account, kept dwelling on her younger sister's assault, even while glossing over her own experiences. It was her son, Abdul, who dropped large hints about that night, and his mother's undisclosed experiences. 'Women in the village sometimes hurl an insult at her or taunt her,' he said.

Abandoned by her husband, yet recognized as no more than a militant's wife whose story must remain suspect, Amira's silence is understandable. It became doubly clear why Amira had played down her own narrative of violence when a journalist-friend revealed that she was carrying a huge burden of responsibility for what had happened to her younger sister. The sister, whose marriage was arranged to someone from another village, continues to suffer from recurrent nightmares. Her in-laws, unaware of her traumatic past, believed that she was possessed by a djinn, especially when she thrashed her hands in the air. Only Amira is privy to the fact that her sister's frantic flailing indicated her return to that night of violence.

◆

---

[37]See *Alleged Perpetrators*, in <http://kashmirprocess.org/reports/alleged_Perpetrators.pdf>, accessed on 9 June 2016.

Whilst the Indian state dismissed Amira's story as fiction, there is documented evidence to show that sexual violence in conflict is very much a part of Kashmir's narrative. A Médecins Sans Frontières report notes its pervasiveness:

> For most Kashmiris sexual violence is considered an inappropriate and difficult to discuss topic. Nevertheless a rather high percentage of respondents—11.6—in comparison to other conflict areas—said they had experienced a violation of their modesty since 1989. [...] Almost two-thirds of the people interviewed (63.9 per cent) had heard over a similar period about cases of rape, while one in seven had witnessed rape.[38]

Added to this are incidents of everyday objectification. In a militarized state, lewd remarks, ogling, wolf whistling, taunting and other forms of sexual harassment are not uncommon. Many of the young girls told me how much they disliked going past checkposts or bunkers and how security personnel often sang out provocative Bollywood ditties. 'If they had been civilian boys or men, we would have taken off our sandals and beaten them. But what do we do with those uniformwallahs?' asked one of them.

Another interviewee told me that shortly after the 2010 protests, his classmate, a girl, appeared terribly disturbed. Apparently, even as protests broke out, troops stormed into a shop where she was buying odds and ends and frisked and groped her persistently. The experience had left her feeling very vulnerable, even helpless.

---

[38]See 'Kashmir: Violence and Health', *Médecins Sans Frontières*, in <https://ru.msf.org/sites/russia/files/migrated/KASHMIR_FINAL_VERSION,_221106.pdf>, accessed on 9 June 2016.

It is not just women who are the victims of sexual violence in the Valley. Male detainees are also susceptible, but their stories have remained largely undocumented. Zahir ud Din, in an article in *Kashmir Reader*, sought to lift the cover on this barely acknowledged crime and—while quoting from an Amnesty International Report of 1992—placed on record that some Kashmiri boys had their sexual organs mutilated during interrogation.[39] The case diaries that the police handed over to the court when they sought to close investigations into the mass rapes of Kunan-Poshpora, too, contained medico-legal reports of burn injuries on a man's sexual organs. Human rights activist Shrimoyee Nandini Ghosh points out that rape, in conflict areas, is also a tool to emasculate men.[40]

◆

Hameeda had agreed to meet me in the Srinagar office of a human rights organization. She travelled alone by a shared Sumo from her home in Kupwara, north Kashmir, dressed in a burqa, that she said, was now her preferred attire while outdoors. She was wary of unwarranted attention and snide remarks—the kind she had been subjected to even recently when a young boy had followed her and asked, 'You're *that* girl, aren't you?'

Inside the office she took off the veil to reveal a strikingly beautiful face. She spoke softly but calmly. Even the *zalzala* (earthquake) that interrupted our conversation did little to faze her.

---

[39]Zahir ud Din, 'Sexual Violence Was Inflicted on Men Too,' *Kashmir Reader*, 22 February 2015.
[40]Shrimoyee Nandini Ghosh, 'Kunan-Poshpora, The Other Story' *Kafila*, in <https://kafila.org/2014/01/20/kunan-poshpora-the-other-story-shrimoyee-nandini-ghosh/>, 20 January 2014, accessed on 10 June 2016.

On 3 July 2004, Hameeda, aged sixteen, was at school when a policeman came in and said she was needed at the police station for interrogation in connection with a murder case in which Hameeda's cousin (a surrendered militant) was a suspect. The school's principal agreed to her being taken to the Zachaldara police station and told her to return after interrogation.

Hameeda told me that at the police post, two women constables beat her, demanding her cousin's whereabouts. A little later, the district superintendent of police (DSP) wished to extract a statement; he asked the women constables to leave the room. Hameeda, alleges that he then made sexual advances, promising to release her if she acquiesced. She spat at him in disgust. He then brought in a common instrument of torture—a roller that is applied on the legs. What followed is unclear.

'I don't really know what happened. I only remember the policeman bearing down on me and kicking me in the groin. I passed out. My next conscious recollection is of seeing my torn uniform and huge bruises on my chest, ' she added.

In the meantime, Hameeda's parents had rushed to the police station and begged for her release. 'My father took the cap off his head, placed it at the officer's feet and pleaded with him to release me. Finally, the police let me go.'

Hameeda was hospitalized. I learnt from a fellow journalist that the medical reports indicated terrible injuries to her sexual organs. (Her ruptured innards suggest she may have been violated even with a baton.)

Over the years, even as Hameeda struggled with her physical injuries, she had to contend with huge emotional trauma. She was often in denial and asked a young woman-journalist whether the act was technically a rape. She hoped that the doctors were mistaken when they said she would never be able to conceive.

Despite great efforts, Hameeda and her family were unable to file an FIR. Instead, the police filed a case against both her and her cousin. Worse, the climate of intimidation destroyed the household's links with support networks. Hameeda recalled, 'Relatives told my mother I was no longer acceptable. My aunt said, "*Yeh humari kuch nahi lagti!* ('She is nobody to us!')"'

Hameeda was viewed as 'spoiled goods', and therefore, as 'fair game'. 'People would come to my father feigning sympathy,' she said, 'and then they'd make indecent proposals. They would say things like, 'Send her to our home and we will give you money.' As a human rights worker observed, Hameeda endures '*zulm*' at two levels—directed at her by the state as well as by society.

Hameeda's own thought process also added to the burden of guilt. She felt responsible for the pain and poverty her parents had to endure. In addition, she felt that she had lost all regard in their eyes. Hameeda confessed to me that her only desire was to withdraw from the world: '*Kissi se bhi baat karna achha nahi lagta* (I don't feel like talking to anyone).'

She had a brief marriage lasting seven months with someone who had police links and abused her sadistically.

Hameeda had approached the SHRC in 2004 when the attack took place. It responded three years later. The Commission members admitted that Hameeda had been subjected to the worst form of human rights violations[41]

[41]http://www.kashmirlife.net/whose-daminis-are-they-16136/; https://authint.com/2014/outpost/asia-pacific/accused-custodial-killing-state-police-official-promotion-in-kashmir-69

(though they did not graphically spell this out). They asked for the indictment of the DSP, and awarded Hameeda ₹75,000 as relief.

When I met her, Hameeda remained torn between continuing a fight for justice and trying to get on with her life and marrying again as her parents were forcing her to do. And, as is often usual in Kashmir, crime was incentivized with the DSP, who is also accused in other human rights violations, being given a President medal, making it even more challenging to go to court.

Later in the day, I attended a session in which a few young professional women, who had formed a support group for rape survivors, spoke to Hameeda. One of her worries was whether her attempts at reclaiming her *izzat* (honour) through marriage would be hindered if she continued with her fight. The participants, in turn, asked her if marriage could possibly bring back her izzat, if she herself did not believe she possessed it. Besides, wouldn't the attempt to claim justice also bring her the izzat she desired?

Pertinently, a month later, a discussion on notions of izzat and understanding of rape took place during the first public address in Srinagar by the villagers of Kunan-Poshpora. In front of a packed hall, on 22 June 2013, the villagers asked why women who had been raped were not being accorded the same status as martyrs. It was, perhaps, for the first time that a discussion on rape as a political weapon was taking place in Kashmir.

◆

Many feminists and human rights activists have pointed out that rape is a part of a wider narrative of race, communal and caste violence and that it has been, systematically, used as a weapon during conflict. A report brought out by Médecins Sans Frontières observes:

> [...] sexual violence is not 'only' a consequence or side effect of war and displacement. It is, instead, a deliberate tool of war, used to destabilize and threaten a part of the civilian population, often a particular group. Women and children are singled out because the harm and humiliation inflicted on them not only hurts them but also deeply harms and humiliates their families and often the entire community.[42]

A UNICEF report, *Sexual Violence as a Weapon of War*, echoes this stance:

> [...the] sexual violation of women erodes the fabric of a community in a way that few weapons can. Rape's damage can be devastating because of the strong communal reaction to the violation and pain stamped on entire families. The harm inflicted in such cases on a woman by a rapist is an attack on her family and culture, as in many societies, women are viewed as repositories of a community's cultural and spiritual values.[43]

Regretfully, while some progress has been made in recognizing rape and other acts of sexual violence as war crimes (rape is now, specifically, mentioned in the Statute of the International Criminal Court), the international and national response remains unclear and inadequate.

Within the context of Kashmir, as early as 1992, a report

---

[42]'Rape as a Weapon of War', *Médecins Sans Frontières*, in <http://www.msf. org/en/article/rape-weapon-war>, 5 March 2004, accessed on 9 June 2016.
[43]See 'Sexual Violence as a Weapon of War', *Unicef*, in <http://www.unicef. org/sowc96pk/sexviol.htm>, accessed on 9 June 2016.

pointed out that rape was being used as a weapon of collective punishment during crackdowns. Indeed, the report went on to state: 'Since most cases of rape take place during cordon-and-search operations, just living in a certain area can put women at risk of rape'[44]—the border areas of Kunan-Poshpora being a prime example. It was also found that rape was being used as a tool for targeting women accused of providing food or shelter to militants (and by extension, accused of being militant sympathizers), and as a means of getting women to identify male relatives as militants.

According to the report—some militant organizations have also been found guilty of targeting women—especially if the women in question are perceived as being informers or if they have been abducted by rival militant groups. An illustration of this was the abduction and murder of a staff nurse called Sarla Bhatt (a member of the Pandit community) of Saura. According to medical investigators, she had been raped. The JKLF claimed responsibility, alleging that she had been informing security troops about the wounded militants admitted in the hospital.

◆

One instance of how a village was called upon to deal with the question of sexual violence perpetrated by militants came my way when I was visiting south Kashmir in 2011. I stopped by at a village (name undisclosed), where I was told that a young woman, Shirin, (name changed) had agreed to speak to me through an intermediary.

---

[44]'Rape in Kashmir: A Crime of War', *Asia Watch: Physicians for Human Rights*, in <https://www.hrw.org/sites/default/files/reports/INDIA935.PDF>, accessed on 9 June 2016.

When she came into the room I was struck by her calm self-possession and joyous countenance. Insisting on the ritual of mehman navaazi, she poured out a cup of *'doodh keva'* (milk tea) and pushed platefuls of green walnuts and ripe pears towards me. Only after these gestures were extended, did she consent to go ahead with the interview. She told me, a little shyly, that the intermediary would narrate her story and that she would then verify details or answer queries.

I learnt that Shirin had been a schoolgirl of fifteen in 2002, when militants abducted her on her way home from school. Just a few days earlier, two militants had sought shelter in her family's home and died in a fierce encounter with the security forces. The senior commander of the Hizb-ul-Mujahideen accused Shirin's father of being an informer and of collaborating with Indian security forces. Hours later, Shirin was abducted in a car with three of his men. Bystanders informed her parents who rushed to the Zainapora police station to lodge a complaint.

One year later, a cowering Shirin was found by the police in a field, holding a small baby boy, even as a fierce gun-battle raged around. The three militants who had abducted her—and who, after repeatedly physically and sexually violating her, had impregnated her—were all killed in this battle.

The three militants, Shirin believed, were foreigners because they would converse with one another in a language she couldn't follow. The police, after taking her statement, closed the case, even while urging Shirin and her community members to put the brutal past behind them. The fact that the perpetrators of violence were dead helped in seeking closure of the case.

The remarkable aspect of Shirin's story was the manner in which her family and village community tried to deal with the complex issues that arose from her abduction, repeated rapes and the birth of her young son. Activists informed me that it was the village elders who decided it was best if Shirin found a groom within the village itself, so that there would be no social stigma. Eventually, the son of the mukhiya married Shirin. Her son, currently, lives with his maternal grandparents and calls Shirin 'sister'—which tactfully 'solves' the problem of providing him legitimacy. Shirin, remains though, emphatically a mother, worrying over whether he was eating enough.

In our brief meeting, Shirin appeared to be comfortable with her partner, with the arrangements made for her son and the fact that both she and her husband could bond with him. It was not clear whether this was a veneer to hide deeper traumas. But as she scooped green walnuts and insisted that I take these gifts back with me, it was clear that Shirin was making every effort to reclaim a life without any kind of resentment.

◆

In conflict zones, sexual violence is often a strategy of intimidation and is employed in flagrant disregard of international human rights norms.

Within Kashmir, when the perpetrators belong to the security forces, even filing a complaint comes with attendant problems—leaving the victims vulnerable to more violence both by perpetrators and by society. Amira was called anti-national; the man who assaulted Hameeda received a state honour; and Pakeeza, to her horror, found that the lure of compensation, which was never given was used to hush up the case and drive a wedge within her family.

Human rights activists—who often urge women to demand

justice for sexual crimes—consequently face a Herculean challenge. Activist Khurram Parvez explained:

'Once, we tried to persuade a woman to file a complaint—she had been raped by a police officer in the presence of her jailed husband. The woman asked us if we could guarantee that she or her husband would not be killed while seeking justice. We couldn't.

'Then there was the *other* question—one that we are always asked. Has a single person from security forces been sentenced? Has justice ever been delivered in this state when the crime has been perpetratred by military personnel? The answer, sadly, is "no". Not a single man from the security forces over the last twenty years or more has been sentenced in Kashmir.' (An Indian Army court did find six of its personnel guilty for the Machil killings on 6 September 2015 and sentenced them to life but the accused were not tried in a civil court.)

It's not surprising then that only a few victims of sexual violence come forward with their stories.

Kashmir's noted human rights lawyer Parvez Imroz, who has been fighting for the reopening of a probe into the Kunan-Poshpora mass rapes, told me the major deterrents to the filing of such cases were the way gender-related allegations were difficult to talk about in a patriarchal society. Also that several gross violations had taken place in rural areas where there is limited access to the media and human rights groups and finally investigations have a poor track record of getting completed.

While AFSPA requires sanction from the Centre to prosecute perpetrators of a crime if they belong to Army ranks, there is no such limitation while conducting investigations. And yet, Imroz reminded me 'that 90 per cent of FIRs have not even been filed, and only in 2 per cent of the cases have investigations been completed'. Even if investigations are completed, the cases remain stuck in the court for years awaiting sanction from the Centre to prosecute under AFSPA. 'People are exhausted fighting cases for over fifteen to twenty years. Many are ill or have died. The next generation does not wish to continue because seeking justice is seen as chasing a mirage. That is a serious challenge before human rights activists and lawyers.'

Yet, narratives of unyielding hope do appear—as in March 2013, when fifty young women came forward and filed a PIL (public interest litigation), demanding a reinvestigation into the Kunan-Poshpora case. Although, the PIL itself was dismissed on the technicality that the police had not actually closed the case, it did help bring the spotlight back on to the episode, with the judicial magistrate of Kupwara directing further investigation. What also followed such legal activism was the formation of a support group for the Kunan-Poshpora survivors. At a public meeting in Srinagar, they spoke out, and the breaking of silence after decades, according to Ather Zia, was a way of taking ownership of the event and recognizing rape as a political weapon.

Zia adds, 'Once this gets reinforced I see a lot of women coming forward. This will take time, of course, and mechanisms will have to be put in place to make things flow in an institutional manner—but yes, I foresee a change.'

Ifrah Butt, one of the young women who pushed for the PIL and later joined the support group, spoke to me about how the idea was born, and why young women, like her, felt morally obliged to demand justice. 'The night of 23–24 February 1991—referred to as a 'Black Day'—could not possibly be forgotten; it remained at the back of our minds. But somehow we did not speak out. Then, as a few of us began thinking of the legal and social ramifications, we saw that this was as much about a group of women suffering, as it was about a land under occupation. This was a struggle, not only for the victims, but for Kashmir. It was time for us to do our bit,' said Ifrah.

This realization came to be echoed by Uzma Qureishi, a student of social work and also one of the petitioners: 'All of us are victims of a certain tyranny. In my particular case, I was once stopped by the forces whilst returning from tuition classes. I was asked to produce my identity card. It hurt and angered me—that I had to prove my identity in my own homeland to the outsiders. This strengthened my resolve to demonstrate solidarity with the women of Kunan-Poshpora.'

These women were linking sexual violence with the overall repression. They were also inspiring an older generation. Ifrah recalled that before the PIL could be admitted the women needed to provide their identity cards. 'I was sitting at home with a bunch of identity cards when my mother asked me what I was doing. I explained everything—our efforts, our demands—and my mother told me to add her name to the PIL. She also wanted to be a part of the struggle.'

Another important outcome was that discussing sexual violence gained legitimacy in a society that, otherwise, viewed such talk as strictly taboo. Ifrah said that at first she could not even use the word 'rape' in front of her father. 'But now *he* tells others that I work with rape survivors. My relatives have accepted the idea that unmarried girls can fight for the rights of those sexually assaulted or meet them during field trips and become friends.'

A similar episode is narrated by activist and social worker Essar Batool. Her family was not only apprehensive when she backed the PIL but there was consternation because the word 'rape' as part of normal parlance was simply not acceptable.

Years ago when Essar's twelve-year-old brother had asked what 'balatkar' (the Hindi word for rape) meant after watching a film on television, her father had mumbled it 'was a very bad thing'.

Now, Essar was using the banned syllable and with impunity! But as she explained to her parents her reasons for backing the PIL, this time the term 'rape' was being employed in its true connotation as a crime and 'as something detached from shame and loss of honour.'

Chapter Six

MAINE NAZIRA, AA KHA?
Memory as Women's Resistance

Parveena Ahangar holds many sobriquets—from Iron Lady to Mother of Kashmir—but she is best known as the founder and chairperson of the Association of Parents of Disappeared Persons (APDP)—which makes her one of the most prominent Kashmiri women in resistance.

It was on a May 2011 morning, with needle-fine rain falling incessantly, that I was first taken to Parveena's home by the young journalist Junaid Rather. The grey sky had drained the landscape of all colour creating a mood of melancholia. Parveena, dressed in black, sat huddled with a kangri. She was unwell but strained her voice to recount her story. It was a tale she had been compelled to tell and retell and yet it had not lost its poignancy.

Parveena spoke of the 1990s. Her son, the seventeen-year-old Javed Ahmad Ahangar, had passed the tenth class and had gone to his uncle's house in Batamaloo where he hoped to pursue further studies. For some days, Parveena was plagued by forebodings, natural perhaps in an era when crackdowns were rampant, but she was particularly disturbed by a black dog in her dreams. It was the early hours of 17 August 1990.

In the morning there was a knock at her door. Parveeena was told that her son, along with three other boys, had been picked up by the National Security Guard personnel and taken to the Hari Niwas interrogation centre. Parveena suspected that the troops were on the lookout for a militant who had the same name as her son and that they picked up Javed, who had a speech impediment, because he had failed to answer questions with alacrity.

More than twenty-six years later, the second-hand accounts of the anguish and terror that her young son underwent before he was taken away, still haunt Parveena. 'I heard he had been stripped. That he was calling out for me and that he desperately wanted a glass of water.'

In the early days after her son's disappearance, a distraught Parveena seesawed between the hope that her son was alive and would be released, and the reality that he had failed to appear even as the other boys were set free. Finally, surfacing from extreme sorrow, she took the first step in the long odyssey of a mother in search of her son and a woman in pursuit of justice.

After an FIR was filed at the Shergari police station and persistent inquiries were made at the Batamaloo branch, Parveena was informed by the Deputy Inspector General that her son had met with an accident, was in the army hospital in Badami Bagh, and would soon be released. When there were no signs of his discharge, she approached the Director General of Police who, in turn, directed her to the Superintendent of Police, in charge of allowing family members to meet detainees. He provided a vehicle for her to visit the hospital. There, an exhaustive search yielded no results. It says much of her early political acumen that she saved the pass she had received at the hospital. This was later proof to show the way a cover-up had been attempted.

Finally, Parveena received crucial information by way of a witness who knew her son. Apparently, he had seen Javed getting beaten by three men near Hari Niwas. This witness went on to offer his testimony when an inquiry was ordered by the court.

What followed was a lengthy court battle over more than two decades in which four petitions were filed. Significantly, despite a court inquiry and report in March 1992 that indicted the alleged perpetrators, the Ministry of Home Affairs refused sanction for prosecution. In 1999, MHA indicated a charge sheet should be filed and sanction could be sought again. But till date no sanction has been given.

Even as legal proceedings dragged on, Parveena hunted for her son, personally, visiting jails and camps in Kashmir, Jodhpur, Hiranagar, Meerut and Delhi (Tihar) and the dreaded interrogation centres like Papa I and Papa II.

While she did not recover her son, she did get a profound understanding of the world of enforced disappearances and the institutionalized denial of justice and custodial violence. Parveena recalled, 'I met so many parents whose sons had suffered enforced disappearances after they were taken away by security troops. I met wives whose husbands had left home and never returned. And I realized that I was not alone.' Empowered by this discovery, Parveena began organizing the families of the missing. They met frequently at a friend's place, in her kitchen and discussed a line of action—for both justice and social welfare. In 1994, the APDP was formed with the help of human rights lawyer Parvez Imroz.[45]

---

[45]Today, there are two separate APDPs—one under Parveena Ahangar and

Soon after this first meeting in Kashmir, I met Parveena in Mumbai where she had come to address a press gathering. I realized why she was called the Iron Lady. Looking pointedly at the audience, she asked why there were separate laws for crimes by Kashmiri civilians and those perpetrated by the army and why those responsible for enforced disappearances and custodial deaths were being granted immunity under AFSPA?

Backing many of her contentions were the SHRC's conclusions in 2011 that there were at least 2,156 anonymous graves across three districts in north Kashmir and that there was 'every possibility that [these...] contain dead bodies of enforced disappearances'.[46] The finding contradicted the state's earlier line that the graves held the remains of foreign militants. Instead, it corroborated what Parveena and reports such as *Buried Evidence* had been asserting. That unidentified dead bodies—many of which bore signs of torture and had been buried by villagers at the behest of the police—were in fact the bodies of those killed in 'encounters and fake encounters' and 'extrajudicial, summary and arbitrary executions'.[47]

The SHRC report hauled up the police for flouting procedures to deal with the unidentified dead. Bashir Ahmed Itoo, the senior superintendent of Police, who led the SHRC investigations, stated that 'human beings have the right not to lose their identity after death, and identification is of

---

the other under Parvez Imroz, who is also the chairman of the JKCCS.

[46]'J&K Human Rights Commission's SIT Confirms 2,156 Unidentified Bodies in "Mass Graves"', *The Hindu*, 22 August 2011.

[47]See *Buried Evidence*, in <http://www.kashmirprocess.org/reports/graves/>, accessed on1 July 2016.

vital importance for police investigation'.[48] Consequently, the SHRC urged the government to embark on the DNA testing of unidentified remains to see if they matched with the DNA of the kin of the missing. But the J&K government claimed it did not have the financial means to conduct such a probe. For Parveena and the families of others like her, this washout meant that they would continue living in an abyss of unknowing. They would never know what happened to their loved ones.

After the Mumbai meeting, I met Parveena a couple of times. What struck me was how effortlessly she moved from the personal space to the political. She was 'Jiji' (the name she is known by in her family and by associates from her days in Batmaloo), lamenting the loss of her son; a friend providing solace to those who grieved like her, besides being a housewife, revealing in a conversation how the prolonged search for a loved one caused friction at home, especially with relatives who insisted that the struggle for justice be abandoned and that she should attend to her household duties. On another level, she was also an activist making steely statements with regard to the situation in Kashmir, the northeast and other regions that had borne witness to violence.

I saw this blurring of spaces when I was at Parveena's home in 2014 and a documentary-film crew was milling around her. Answering their questions, she revealed details about her son—how close he was to his sister Saima (who now works in the APDP); how he planned to learn typing after his matriculation and how he was an ordinary boy with humble aspirations. She then switched seamlessly to the facts

---

[48]See 'Digging Out the Truth', *The Times of India: Crest*, 3 December 2011, by the author of this book.

surrounding her fight for justice—how she refused relief of over 1 lakh rupees because, her aim was not to earn money but to fight for justice. She said she had refused the CNN-IBN Indian of the Year Award in 2011,[49] because accepting it seemed farcical, given that there had been no formal response from the Indian Government on the issue of enforced disappearances. She disagreed with the citation of the award that claimed her actions had forced the Centre to respond to gross human rights violations. It was patently false as long as thousands of cases revolving around enforced disappearances languished in the Srinagar High Court.

Parveena's commitment to her cause has helped the APDP broaden its kin-based activism, and find support while taking up issues like judicial torture and the plight of half-widows— for whom medical help and emotional support is offered.

Her trajectory from victim to activist has inspired other half-widows to rebuild their lives. I learnt of Shazia (name changed) who fought to educate her children who now are actively pursuing their careers, and that she is constructing a new house. The APDP, under Parveena, has helped create a sea-change in the way Kashmir's women are perceived— strong entities even as they mourn.

Most of all, Parveena's activism has helped Kashmir not to forget.

◆

Her quest to keep the 'missing' in Kashmir's collective consciousness is visible during the silent sit-ins in Pratap Park

---

[49]See 'Parveena Ahangar Rejects CNN-IBN's Nomination for Indian of the Year 2011', *Kafila*, in <https://kafila.org/2011/12/11/parveena-ahangar-rejects-cnn-ibns-nomination-for-indian-of-the-year-2011/>, accessed on 4 July 2016.

on the tenth of every month. These sit-ins, that have captured Kashmir's imagination, are reminiscent of the weekend demonstrations by women in Istanbul's Galatasaray to invoke the names of those who had suffered enforced disappearances in Turkey after the 1980 coup d'état; or the protests by Madres de (Mothers of) la Plaza de Mayo of Argentina to draw attention to those who had 'vanished' during the 'Dirty War.'

In Pratap Park, protesters, most of whom are women, accompanied by their children or other relatives, sit with photographs of missing members. Sometimes they clutch these photos to their heart; at other times they tenderly caress the faces in the pictures; occasionally, they arrange prints in a montage. There is mourning and loud weeping. There are 'maternal, non-threatening, informal practices of grief'[50]— singing snatches of a lullaby, or displaying of old clothes and belongings that had been lovingly hoarded and preserved.

These creative visual practices and the 'nature of sight and seeing' have been analysed by Deepti Misri, an assistant professor of Women and Gender Studies at the University of Colorado, Boulder. She spoke to me of her anthropological interest in these sit-ins that magnified the power of protests. While the state rendered 'invisible' stories of enforced disappearances and custodial killings, the APDP countered the official narrative by its 'visual appropriation' of a prominent expanse like Pratap Park. Here, the deliberate movement of grief 'into the public visual sphere' redirects the gaze of tourists, passersby, Kashmiris themselves and not the least the state itself. [51]

---

[50]In the words of anthropologist Ather Zia, who spent many years working with the families of those who had disappeared in Kashmir.
[51]Deepti Misri, *Beyond Partition: Gender Violence and Representation in Postcolonial India* (Illinois: University of Illinois Press, 2014).

Deepti has also written about the way the largely male photographers choose to focus their lens not so much on the men, who also form part of APDP sit-ins, but on the grieving women because of the arresting visuals they make.

◆

Many of the mourners at Pratap Park have become well-known names—like the late Mughli, affectionately known as Mughli-maasi.

A much-loved figure, Mughli was one of the oldest members of the APDP. Deserted by her husband, she brought up her son Nazir Ahmad Teli as a devoted single parent and shared a unique bond with him. Nazir grew up to become a teacher. On 1 September 1990, the thirty-five-year-old set out for school. He never returned. Like so many of the Valley's grieving parents, Mughli went down a path of endless investigation and exhausted all legal options. At the silent protests she would capture the attention of bystanders with her intense conversations with her son, affectionately crooning to him and thus making a most poignant effort to keep him alive.

Upon Mughli's death on 27 October 2009, journalist Shazia Yousuf, in a moving tribute, wrote of her last public sit-in on 10 June.[52] Clad in a simple cotton pheran, Mughli had appeared listless, sometimes tearing at her hair in despair. She had not brought along the photograph of her son. Four months later, she died in hospital.

In her final moments (according to close sources), she

[52]Shazia Yousuf, 'When Mughli Lost Her Only Friend and Companion,' *Greater Kashmir*, in <http://www.risingkashmir.com/news/when-mughli-lost-her-only-friend-and-companion>, 6 February 2015, accessed on 7 July 2016.

murmured, *'Maine Nazira, aa kha?'*—'My Nazira, you have come?' Her conversations with her son persisted to the very end. Her mission to find him remained alive till her last breath.

Ather Zia, who also wrote on Mughli, observed how she was much more than a *mater dolorosa*, a sorrowful mother. Rather—to quote Parveena—she imparted valuable lessons in remembering those who disappeared, through lamentation. What can one make of the politics of mourning? Ather comments that the work of 'mourning [focuses] on giving birth to a memory.'[53]

She adds that grieving may seem instinctive and biological—no more than an anguished search for someone lost—but it is in fact 'a deeply political quest, which requires rigour, passion, strategy, motivation, initiative and a sense of brave invincibility against extreme threats to life under coercive laws.'[54] It is, in truth, 'performative politics'— Kashmiri mothers using their bodies as a theatrical site at monthly sit-ins. Such displays may not conform to the tenets of Western feminism but, in the Valley, actively assuming the identity of a mother/wife looking for a child/husband becomes nothing less than a radical statement.

Feminist Nivedita Menon too has discussed how women use their conventional identities in creative ways to become activists. She quotes Malathi de Alwis on the 'subversive maternalist politics' employed by The Mother's Front in Sri Lanka—a group protesting against enforced disappearances in the island nation in the 1990s. Each woman presented herself in the traditional role of a mother and invoked maternal

---

[53]http://www.kashmirlit.org/remembering-mugli-human-rights-activist/
[54] Ather Zia, *The Spectacle of a Good Half-Widow: Performing Agency in the Human Rights Movement in Kashmir* (California: UCLA Center for the Study of Women, 2013).

suffering—but each simultaneously subverted the idea of a mother as the custodian of a private identity by expressing deeply felt sentiments in public arenas, marching through the streets and confronting the Sri Lankan state.[55]

Ather Zia went on to study how Sadaf, a half-widow and a mother of three sons aligned herself with the politics of performance by assuming the identity of an *asal zanan* (a good woman who is obedient, listens, dresses modestly and remains invisible)—while simultaneously pushing, ever so subtly, the boundaries of the term so that it could accommodate activism. During a sit-in, Sadaf wore a voluminous scarf covering most of her face; her gaze remained downcast. She held a photo of her husband, Manzoor, with a written statement: 'Half-widow—return my disappeared husband.' New bystanders were compelled to ask: 'Who is this woman? Why does she mourn publicly, yet choose to remain hidden? Really, what is she making visible and invisible at the same time?' Ather analyses the nuanced attempt at raising awareness about enforced disappearances and the phenomenon of half-widows, while remaining acutely conscious of social and political constraints in a patriarchal and violent space.

Sadaf's public statement in mourning is brought about by a personal history where slander replaced sympathy. As a half-widow she had to hear comments about her naturally rosy complexion being the result of 'makeup'; she was subjected to sexual harassment when an Ikhwani tried stalking her. When she started wearing a burqa to counter everyday debasement, rumours began swirling that she was an informer in disguise. The burqa, too, had to be abandoned. Sadaf's brothers also had begun exerting pressure on her to get married again.

---

[55]Nivedita Menon, *Seeing Like a Feminist* (New Delhi: Penguin, 2012), p. 170.

Sadaf found herself surrounded by men exerting control over her, telling her what to do. 'They all became my husband, even those militarywallahs,' was her pithy observation. In this violence-ridden and deeply patriarchal community, Sadaf chose to play the role of an *asal zanan*—complete with demure attire and muted responses—but a performance that acccomodated the steely activism and memorialization she was actually practising.[56]

◆

The French philosopher Michel Foucault states:

> Since memory is a very important factor in struggle (really, in fact, struggles develop a kind of conscious moving forward of history), if one controls people's memory, one controls their dynamism. And one also controls their experience, their knowledge of the previous struggles.[57]

Kashmir seems to have absorbed the significance of this observation—as I found when I visited Shopian. The town— its name derived from 'sheeyan' or 'place of snow'—stands testimony to the ways in which Kashmir has resisted all attempts to alter or erase its experiences.

In 2011, I was struck by the way young women in Shopian continued to seethe over the state's narrative about the deaths of Asiya and Neelofar, two women who were found dead in the waters of the Rambi Ara Nallah. The women of Shopian

---

[56] Ather Zia, *The Spectacle of a Good Half-Widow: Performing Agency in the Human Rights Movement in Kashmir* (California: UCLA Center for the Study of Women, 2013).

[57] 'Film in Popular Memory: An Interview with Michel Foucault,' *The Collective Memory Reader*, edited by Jeffrey K. Olick, Vered Vinitzky-Seroussi and Daniel Levy (UK: Oxford University Press, 2011), pp. 252-253.

asserted that the two did not accidentally drown as the state claimed but were raped and murdered by the security forces. Asma, a young teacher told me, 'When I saw Neelofar's photograph in the newspapers, I recalled having seen her at a tailor's shop—she had come to pick up her husband's clothes. All of us, as women, felt we had to do something. We organized demonstrations. We participated in protests. We did all we could. But justice is yet to be done.'

That memories still live on is evident in a 'wall memorial' that has been erected near the graveyard of the two women—paying homage not just to Asiya and Neelofar, but to all those who have suffered sexual violence by the security forces.

It is also evident in Arshad Mushtaq's poem titled 'That's When I Threw Stones', which connects the heartache and repression of Kashmir's women's across time with the tragedy that unfolded along the waters of Rambi Ara Nallah. Mushtaq does this without even mentioning Asiya and Neelofar's names:

> *When they left Lal Ded naked*
> *On the bank of the Rambiar,*
> *When they killed Yousuf before Zooni's eyes*
> *That's when I threw stones.*[58]

---

[58]'It was the Mughal emperor Akbar who deposed and exiled Habba Khatoon, or Zooni's husband, and Kashmir's ruler, Yusuf, to Bihar where he eventually died. [Aga] Shahid [Ali] had written in "A Prologue", how it was since Akbar's act of imperial injustice, Kashmir ceased to be free. He also writes how it was Habba Khatoon's grief—"alive to this day"—that "roused the people into frenzied opposition to Mughal rule".' See Manash Bhattacharjee, 'Review: Of Gardens and Graves by Suvir Kaul', in <http://therumpus. net/2015/07/of-gardens-and-graves-by-suvir-kaul/ >, 3 July 2015, accessed on 4 July 2016.

◆

Yet, with the fading away of an older generation several narrative threads are at the risk of getting lost. Parveena spoke to me movingly of how when Gul Mohammed, an elderly man seeking justice, was dying, he took her hand, placed it on his head and said, 'You are my sister and I am passing on my mission to you.' Even while accepting his struggle as her own, Parveena remains conscious of how to keep the torch burning. How does one keep memory, as a form of resistance, alive?

Several APDP volunteers, battling similar concerns, try keeping a legacy of recollections intact. An APDP volunteer, now in her eighties, has begun bringing along her granddaughter to sit-ins. Yet, another family organizes cricket tournaments in the memory of their lost one.

Kashmir's youth are resurrecting their tortured past and also drawing creative inspiration from the various movements when aligning with the arts. These include rap singers like M.C. Kash and Shayan Nabi to authors like Shahnaz Bashir who has written a novel titled *The Half Mother*.[59] Artist Malik Sajad sketches in his sensitivity to enforced disappearances in his graphic book, *Munnu: A Boy from Kashmir*[60], and one of his earlier sketches of a hand across a barbed wire, shrouded, with three fingers missing, has been modified for use as the logo of the APDP. Filmmaker Iffat Fatima has documented the lives of women who lost their husbands or sons in enforced disappearances in powerful films like *Where Have You Hidden My New Crescent Moon* and *Blood Leaves Its Trail*.

Arshad Mushtaq's poignant play *Be'te Chius Shahid*

---

[59]Shahnaz Bashir, *The Half Mother* (New Delhi: Hachette, 2014).
[60]Malik Sajad, *Munnu: A Boy from Kashmir* (New Delhi: HarperCollins, 2015).

(I am also a witness)—a reading of letters to emphasize the inheritance of loss—that I saw being performed at Pratap Park during an APDP sit-in—is an illustration of how a public 'postmemory'[61] is being constructed.

In downtown Srinagar, in a building that hosts computer classes, young boys and girls, under the guidance of A. Naqshab, meet informally, bringing with them their varied interests in poetry, music, dramatics, and videography to build distinct narratives about Kashmir's past. One of the key projects of the downtown volunteers has been creating profiles by stitching together oral histories of those in the martyrs' graveyard.

Saima, one of the downtown volunteers, has demonstrated her generation's solidarity with the women of Kunan-Poshpora through a play that critiques an intolerant society. Ansur Farrukh Khan has dwelt on Kashmir's legendary freedom fighter Maqbool Bhat through a production that examines him from two conflicting perspectives—Maqbool, the terrorist, and Maqbool, the martyr.

Shazia Yousuf, as a journalist, too ferrets out stories of a deeply fractured society where the neat labels of victim and perpetrator cannot be applied. She has written about the lives of women married to the despised Ikhwanis—women who had little control over the decisions of their husbands—and had to negotiate the murky ground between 'traitorousness

---

[61]'Postmemory' is term coined by Holocaust scholar Marianne Hirsch, to describe 'the relationship that later generations or distant contemporary witnesses bear to the personal, collective, and cultural trauma of others—to experiences they "remember" or know only by means of stories, images, and behaviours.' See Marianne Hirsch, *Connective Histories in Vulnerable Times*, in <https://apps.mla.org/pdf/2014_pres_address_pmla.pdf>, accessed on 14 July 2016.

and family loyalty'[62].

Uzma Falak explores through her camera and her power of words the ability to mould time into a political tool. She was fifteen, when Inayat, the physically-challenged, musically-gifted son of one of her close relatives, was killed while taking a walk outside his home in Munawarabad near a CRPF camp. This was when she first engaged with language as a means of remembrance.

Her poem, titled *Gasoline Rainbow*, freezes memory of her grandmother's home, razed to the ground during an encounter between militants and security forces. 'I have very warm recollections of my nanihal's house,' Uzma told me, 'which was in a quiet suburb of Srinagar. Our own home had no garden, no open spaces, so my nanihal's house was doubly special.' Architecturally, too, I'm told, it was magnificent, with 'Khatamband'[63]. After the razing, Uzma was not permitted to visit the space—her mother feared that it would upset her daughter far too much.

The yearning to see what happened to her beloved nanihal's residence persisted, and in 2012, Uzma finally made a visit with her camera. 'I tried to find objects that I could identify,' she said. The dwelling had been rebuilt, it was entirely different. 'In my dreams, though, I still see the old house—just as it was, each corner.' Her poem *Gasoline Rainbow* reads:

---

[62]*Garrisoned Minds: Women and Armed Conflict in South Asia*, Edited by Laxmi Murty and Mitu Varma.
[63]Khatamband is a rare Kashmiri art, where small pieces of wood (preferably walnut or deodar) are connected in geometrical patterns, without the use of nails, to form a ceiling.

We children would tip-toe
on the intricate patterns on the carpet
Trying not to tread on a different colour
Tracing red, for example
Till our toes became fingers of the weaver
and
In our hearts we praised the dexterous weaver
as we looked in awe at his dream.

Patterns then dissolved and
colours became transparent
We saw our faces,
our rainbow of threads
in the puddle of dreams
away from
the gasoline rainbow

When they burnt my Grandma's house,
the old wooden man, my drawing of a mermaid under the carpet,
the Khatamband squares, radio,
the Famous Five Series and the elegant Arabic calligraphy
all turned to ash
as I write this I realize,
memories always surface even from the deepest rubble
like the promise of resurrection

My mind is a trellis
where
the ivy grows
inconsolably.[64]

---

[64]See *Gasoline Rainbow, Kindle Magazine,* in <http://kindlemag.in/gasoline-rainbow/>, accessed on 4 July 2016.

Uzma reminded me how, in Kashmir, time takes on a malleable quality—shaping and reshaping itself—to create enduring histories.

Chapter Seven

UMEED HAI
Women Seeking Justice in Kashmir

During a particularly dank week in May, it struck me as significant that two different sets of women were protesting in Srinagar and memorializing events, oblivious to the cold and rain. While Parveena's silent sit-in focussed on enforced disappearances, Anjum Zamrud Habib and her allies were on the streets drawing attention to another section of Kashmiri society that has gone missing—the thousands incarcerated in jails, either booked under the dreaded PSA or awaiting trial.

Zamrud is no stranger to the ordeals of prison life. Besides her association with the MKM, what is important is her experience as Qaidi (Prisoner) Number 100 during her five years in Tihar Jail. She had been arrested under the Prevention of Terrorism Act (POTA)[65] on 6 February 2003, after she had gone to the Pakistani embassy in Delhi for a visa. It was alleged that she had cash in her possession—which she maintained

---

[65]'The law provides for capital punishment for terrorist killings, ninety days of detention without trial and special courts to deal with terrorist cases.' See 'POTA Bill Passed by Joint Session of Parliament', *Rediff*, in <http://www.rediff.com/news/2002/mar/26poto7.htm>, accessed on 8 July 2016.

had been collected to buy computers for an orphanage—and was acting as conduit for illegitimate transfers.

Lodged in a dark cell with no natural light, in Barrack Number 4 of the female ward of Tihar, Zamrud was not accorded the status of a political prisoner. She was jailed with criminals who, she said, took pleasure in beating and taunting newcomers, particularly Muslim women. She had to contend with policemen who, she claimed, abused her; doctors who remained reluctant to examine her and staff who exhibited signs of communal prejudice. On her first night in prison, when she asked for water, she recalled that she was told to take it from the toilet.

Zamrud draws attention not just to her own experiences but to blatant human rights abuses in Indian jails. She narrates how inmate Zohra died on being violently punched in jail, of how prisoners once waited helplessly while a fire raged in the barracks ('It was as if they [the prison staff] wanted us to burn alive that day,' Zamrud said) and the day when a convict hanged herself from the fan and died. In all this, she learnt a valuable life-lesson: 'I was not the lone sufferer.' And that, 'Every Kashmiri lodged in jail struggles.'

These contentions have been backed by investigations, such as the one conducted by the Jammu and Kashmir Bar Association that holds that custodial deaths are very much of a reality in the state;[66] or the report by Amnesty that highlights that the PSA is a 'lawless law' that allows people to get booked and detained merely on the charge that they are a possible

---

[66]'In January 1997, the Jammu and Kashmir Bar Association documented 218 deaths in custody in 1996. All had reportedly been arrested first and then killed in detention centres inside or outside the state.' See <http://www.refworld.org/pdfid/3ae6a99a4.pdf>, accessed on 8 July 2016.

threat to public life.[67]

Upon her release on bail, Zamrud, drawing strength from the Geneva Convention that endorses the rights of detainees, headed the Association of Families of Kashmiri Prisoners (AFKP). The association which fervently advocates a data-based study of the number of custodial killings and prison rights violations in Kashmir, has taken up the cause of inmates without adequate defence, those from penurious backgrounds or those languishing without trial.

It is Zamrud who drew attention to the case of prisoner Farooq Khan, a graduate from Chennai employed with Kashmir's Public Health Engineering Department, who was accused of the 1996 Delhi blasts.[68] At meetings and conferences, Farooq's mother and Zamrud would speak up for this young engineer. They reminded audiences of the manner of his arrest—maintaining that he was picked up by Ikhwanis and then arrested by the Special Task Force (STF). They asserted that while wasting away in various jails in Kashmir and other parts of India as an under-trial, he had lost precious years of his life. They drew attention to a letter Farooq wrote to his brother after twelve years in jail, where he commented that his time as an undertrial almost equalled a life sentence of fourteen years.[69] Farooq was eventually acquitted and released in September 2014 by a court in Rajasthan.

Apart from taking up the cause of inmates, the AFKP,

[67]A "Lawless Law"', *Amnesty*, in <http://www.amnestyusa.org/sites/default/files/asa200012011en_11.pdf>, accessed on 8 July 2016.

[68]Uzma Falak, 'In Search of Lost Time, *Himal*, in <http://himalmag.com/in-search-of-lost-time-kashmir-incarceration/?currentPage=all>, 12 September 2015, accessed on 8 July 2016.

[69]'Indian Court Acquits Kashmiri Engineer After 18 Years', *Kashmir Media Service*, in <http://www.kmsnews.org/news/2014/09/30/indian-court-acquits-kashmiri-engineer-after-18-years.html>, accessed on 8 July 2016.

undertakes rehabilitation efforts, offers counselling to ex-detainees and renders help to the families of ex-convicts suffering from isolation.

Such outreach is especially commendable given how hard it is to find volunteering support from released male detainees. *'Ghar mein pareshani hai aur humme kamana hai'*('We are in financial distress and must earn money')—that's what they tell me,' Zamrud revealed. 'Here's where I think gender differences come into play. I, as a woman, emerged from jail believing that it was imperative for me to empathize with those going through a similar ordeal, and act—despite the fact that my mother worried that I would be rearrested if I protested.'

Zamrud's tone was matter-of-fact. She refused to indulge in rancour or bitterness. Nor would she let herself sink into an abyss of self-pity, even as she exhibited defiance, *'Mein itni kamzor nahi ki mein meri daastan ro ro ke kahoon'* (I'm not so feeble that I will narrate my story with tears.) The resilience shines through in a book she authored on her time in prison.[70] She told me how during her book launch in Kashmir, she announced in front of a packed hall, 'Don't use the epithet *bechaari* (someone to be pitied). Call me instead *tehreek nawaazi* (someone who loves the movement).'

As I left Zamrud's company, she declared, like only a *tehreek nawaazi* could, 'They can physically incarcerate us... but they can't shackle our minds.'

◆

---

[70]Anjum Zamrud Habib, *Prisoner No. 100: An Account of My Nights and Days in an Indian Prison* (New Delhi: Zubaan, 2011). The book is based on a journal she kept in prison and recounts the hostility she faced as a woman, a Kashmiri and a Muslim.

'What need we fear who knows it, when none can call our power to account?'[71] For legal activist Ashok Agrwaal, this line from *Macbeth* sums up the justice system in Kashmir and how Constitutional guarantees become deadwood when the state cannot be held accountable.

The 'impossibility of justice' in J&K is the premise of his monograph, *In Search of Vanished Blood: The Writ of Habeas Corpus in Jammu and Kashmir, 1990–2004*,[72] which dwells on how draconian laws like AFSPA and the PSA and impunity have crippled the judiciary. Agrwaal observes on the enervated state of judicial institutions:

> The single most-striking feature of the *habeas corpus* proceedings is the powerlessness of the High Court. Everything else can be derived from this fact. From the point of time when the court issued *notice* of the petition upon the respondents, it lost all control over the proceedings. The pace, the manner in which the case would proceed and the outcome of the case was controlled entirely by the respondents: the Central and the state governments.[73]

He also notes that 'amnesiac functioning' of the courts has allowed unscrupulous respondents and lawyers to get away with years of delay in filing replies and inveigling the court to dispose off petitions in the absence of representation on behalf of petitioners.

---

[71]William Shakespeare, *Macbeth*, Act 5, Scene 1.

[72]Ashok Agrwaal, *In Search of Vanished Blood: The Writ of Habeas Corpus in Jammu and Kashmir, 1990–2004* (Kathmandu: South Asia Forum for Human Rights Paper Series 17, 2008).

[73]*Ibid.* See also Ashok Agrwaal, 'Judicial Indifference to Deaths in Custody or "Disappearances"', *South Asia Citizens Web*, in <http://www.sacw.net/article29.html>, 14 September 2008, accessed on 12 July 2016.

Agrwaal's indictment then begs the question—who is brave enough to pursue a case for years on end?

I found an answer on a rain-soaked Friday in the first week of September 2014, when I called up Munawara Sultan and asked for an update regarding the hearing of her case. She told me that there would be no hearing that day; large areas of Srinagar were getting water-logged, and judges and lawyers had expressed their inability to attend court. On her part, Munawara was perfectly willing to walk through knee-deep water, if need be, to keep intact her unblemished record of attending every hearing in a case she had filed against the security troops for the death of her husband in the 1990s.

Two days after our conversation, the Jhelum engulfed Srinagar and effectively shut down the Valley for more than a month. The paralysis imposed by nature was an ironic reflection of the torpor of justice mechanisms in the state.

A week before the flood, I had visited Munawara at her home in Batamaloo to learn more about her resilience in the face of a *tareek pur tareek* (date after date) judicial stalemate. In her room there hung a large framed photograph of a handsome man sporting a beret-like cap ('pakol') with his arm tenderly around a woman. That, explained Munawara, was a picture taken shortly after her wedding to Gowhar Amin. Her son, Anis, who I met later, bore a striking resemblance to the father, carrying his light eyes. The age of the boy—twenty-three years—matched the number of years Munawara has devoted of her life to fighting the case.

Going back in time she said, 'I was married on 2 December 1992. The wedding got postponed because of the haalat.' It was the height of the militancy and Batamaloo, a stronghold of militants, was rocked by violence, clampdowns and curfews.

Four months after her wedding, Munawara went back

with her husband to her parents' home for Id celebrations and a dawat (feast). During the visit, on 7 April 1993, there was a mine blast near a bus stand in the locality and some BSF personnel were killed. The area was cordoned off.

Early the next morning, on 8 April 1993, a call went out from the mosque for male members to assemble at the bus stand for an identification parade. Gowhar too took his position in this routine drill—whereby male members had to come forward before a Gypsy within which sat mukhbirs (informers) and troops.

'To my mind, my husband made one fatal mistake,' said Munawara. 'He had spotted a tap and bucket, and began offering water to men who had been waiting in a line since 4 a.m. without food or drink. This led to an altercation with the jawans who objected to his "crime" of offering people water.'

At around 11 a.m., a key member of the fourth battalion of the BSF arrived with his deputy and, according to Munawara, in the presence of hundreds of eye-witnesses, bundled Gowhar into the Gypsy and took him away.

Munawara recalled, 'We were waiting at home. At around 3 p.m., we heard three gunshots. We wondered where they were coming from. After the cordon was lifted at around 5 p.m., people began making their way back home. When my husband did not make an appearance, my father went to the police control room. Even as the police were reassuring my father that my husband would return, two bodies were brought in.'

One of those dead was Gowhar, with bullet wounds on the head and chest. It later emerged that he had been taken to Banpura in Batamaloo, to a cowshed, where he was shot. To Munawara's father, it was clear that Gowhar had been killed at close range. A pregnant Munawara, aged twenty, was plunged into widowhood.

Munawara described her loss: 'I knew the joys of being a bride for four months. My husband would never see his unborn child. My son was fated to never know a father's love. I was deprived of a husband. Three lives were irrevocably affected. It wasn't *one* person who died that day in this family, but *three*.'

After the customary four days of mourning, she, along with her family, tried to file an FIR of abduction and murder against the BSF—not an easy task in the nineties, since the police were intimidated by the armed forces. In Munawara's instance, it took the intervention of a chief judicial magistrate (CJM) for an FIR to be filed on 20 April, almost a fortnight after Gowhar's death.[74]

In the meantime, the BSF had lodged a case before Munawara's family could, claiming that two unidentified militants, who had attacked a search party during a cordon operation, had been killed in retaliatory firing; some arms and ammunition had been recovered from the spot. One of the militants was identified as Gowhar.

Munawara, who takes personal interest in the details of the case, argued that the FIR filed by the BSF was the first big lie in a saga of untruths. 'What followed were multiple contradictory statements. Sometimes the claim was that two men were shot during cross-firing; sometimes, it was suggested that the bodies were found lying on the road and brought in. To date, the BSF has not been able to produce the arms that they claimed they found on the 'militants'. Besides,

---

[74]See 'HC Opens 1993 Custodial Killing Case', *Kashmir Awareness*, in <http://www.kashmirawareness.org/hc-reopens-1993-custodial-killing-case-2/>, 4 June 2010, accessed on 12 July 2016.

the diaries of the police control room do not have any record of untoward incidents of firing that day.'

Over the years, the fight for justice became increasingly complex as there were a slew of petitions related to the case that Munawara had to actively pursue. The police had even closed the file, then reopened it but not made any progress in investigations. In 2003, another petition was then filed asking for completion of investigations and ex gratia payment.

Munawara had also approached the SHRC on 21 October 2003 and when summoned, told the SHRC panel, in her inimitable way, that she wanted a quick decision since she was tired and had worn out her pair of sandals from running about. The decision on 4 October 2006 by the SHRC was unequivocal:

> Gowhar Amin Bahadur was lifted by 4th Bn of BSF during cordon and was killed in custody. […] The unfortunate part of the case, therefore, is that BSF party have not made themselves accountable before the investigation of the case.'[75]

The SHRC recommended ex gratia payment of 2 lakh rupees and employment on compassionate grounds as stipulated under the Statutory Rules and Orders.

Armed with the order, Munawara filed another petition in the High Court, asking for ex gratia, employment and further compensation/damages of ₹1 lakh as well as completion of investigations. The Deputy Commissioner though chose to go by the BSF version and refused to comply. The High Court,

---

[75]See Arif Shafi Wani, 'After 13 Years, Widow from Batmaloo Gets Some Justice,' *Greater Kashmir*, in <http://www.greaterkashmir.com/news/news/after-13-years-widow-from-batmaloo-gets-some-justice/14035.html>, 7 November 2006, accessed on 11 July 2016.

on 31 May 2010, then directed the CJM to probe and submit a fresh inquiry report.

This inquiry meant there were now two courts' proceedings that Munawara had to attend. Often she shuttled from one to the other on the same day. Finally, CJM Yashpaul Bournuey, in his report submitted to the High Court, said:

> I am of the considered view that the accusations made by the applicant are well-founded and substantiated. She [Munawara Sultan] has produced eye-witnesses who all are local inhabitants of the area, and have categorically stated that Gowhar was lifted by BSF men in their presence and few hours later his body was handed over to police.[76]

Further, he stated that the stand of the BSF 'does not appear to be true on face. The investigating agency has also played its part by sleeping over the matter for almost two decades and has miserably failed to collect vital clues.'[77]

However, it took a contempt notice for non-implementation of this ruling and strong words by the High Court before the DC made payment of ex gratia and compensation, and her son Anis was provided employment in a government office. For Munawara, this only brought partial relief. 'Had his father been alive, Anis would still be studying,' she told me.

What Munawara really sought was justice following the reinvestigation ordered by the CJM and the High Court. But the case remains stuck in a cruel impasse.

The police on 17 April 2013 in the status report claimed

---

[76]'18-yr-old's Custodial Death Case,' *Kashmir Watch*, in <http://kashmirwatch. com/18-yr-olds-custodial-death-case/>, 11 July 2011, accessed on 12 July 2016.
[77]Ibid.

they were seeking sanction from the Centre to prosecute. But a right to information plea revealed that no such request has been sent.

Summing up this case *Alleged Perpetrators* notes:

> [The case of Gowhar's killing is] a strong indictment of the various processes of justice. A case of 1993 remains pending with limited progress except for payment of ₹1 lakh ex gratia. This notwithstanding a confirmation by the SHRC, the CJM Srinagar and the High Court that the victim was abducted by the Fourth Battalion, BSF. [...] A case of gruesome human rights violations has been allowed to remain pending for nineteen years due to the all pervasive culture of impunity.[78]

Every turn in this legal labyrinth has meant mental pain and physical stress for Munawara. She has come face-to face with those whom she believes are responsible for her husband's killing and has rejected offers to drop the case. In the early days, she had a member of her family by her side, but now, confidently fights legal battles on her own.

She also chose economic independence by selling her jewellery and purchasing two autorickshaws which she gives out on hire. She built a house for herself and her son by persuading her father to give her a portion of the land he owned. 'Did you notice the nameplate near the gate of my home?' she asked me with maternal pride. 'It bears my son's name!'

What amazes me about Munawara is not just her strength but also her commitment to making the case a personal mission.

---

[78]*Alleged Perpetrators*, in <http://kashmirprocess.org/reports/alleged_ Perpetrators.pdf>, accessed on 9 June 2016.

She has attended every hearing, no matter how unwell she is or how bad the weather. She has familiarized herself with the workings of the judicial system. Her comprehension of the details of the case impresses her lawyers. She has an evolved grasp of the language of human rights and a keen political awareness. 'Why are there special laws for crimes committed in Kashmir when it is repeatedly said that Kashmir is an integral part of Hindustan?' is the question she often asks.

What makes her so tenacious? What gives her the strength to declare: 'I will go to any corner of the world to get justice; I will die fighting?'

Is it her faith that makes her declare, '*Umeed hai* (I have hope). The truth cannot be hidden. If I am with the truth, I will get justice. And, Inshallah, I will always be with the truth?'

Is it a firm spiritual ethos that reveals itself when she makes statements like: '*Subse bada court upar walle ke haath mein hai. Magar idhar hamme haath-paun hilana padega."* ('The Almighty runs the biggest court. But it is incumbent on us to fight for justice.)

Does her view that seeking justice is a divine mission stem from her faith in Islam? And is that how she gains the understanding that 'the politics of the faithful is a kind of prayer'?[79]

Or, is some of this resolve linked to her love for her son? Munawara spoke of how she had to step into the shoes of an absent father. When Anis was little, she would accompany him to male-dominated barber shops or run behind him while he tried to cycle. Her father too tried to make sure the boy would not lack the affectionate gifts of a father and would

---

[79]A quote by Shaykh Muhammad Hussein Fadlallah in Upendra Baxi, *The Future of Human Rights* (New Delhi: Oxford University Press, 2008), p. 193.

buy him chocolates and chewing gum. For years, the boy believed his grandfather to be his father.

'One day he asked, 'Why does my father have such few teeth?' And I teasingly replied, 'Don't you remember how you gave him a blow and knocked some of them off?'

Yet when Anis was thirteen, and kept asking about his middle name—Gowhar—there could be no more prevarication. Munawara revealed the truth, and the boy she had spent a lifetime protecting 'literally became weak'. Munawara told me that for all that had been stolen from him—a father, siblings, childhood innocence—she owed him justice. 'Our struggle is for the next generation,' she said, 'so that they have a *khushaali zindagi* (joy-filled life). The injustices I suffered are not repeated. What I had to undergo—that should not happen to our children.'

Chapter Eight

WHERE ELSE CAN I GO?
Women, Spirituality and the Valley

'Let's visit the shrines this afternoon,' suggested Mahum. It was April 2015, and spring—which had been in suspended animation was now reassuring us with glints of sunshine breaking through the grey clouds.

We reached the Khanqah of Shah Hamdanor Khanqah-i-Mualla, as it is popularly known, just before Friday prayers were coming to a close. Built in a synthesis of Central Asian architectural traditions and indigenous elements, this stunning shrine with wooden mouldings and hanging bells, resembles a pagoda. Instead of the dome, there is a bronze and gold spire that is described by author Mirza Waheed as 'God's own earring adorned with black pearls'.[80]

The shrine's history is as compelling as its architecture—constructed in 1395 by Sultan Sikander in honour of Mir Sayed Ali Hamdani, the prominent Sufi poet from Persia who came to Kashmir in 1375 with 700 followers to escape the persecution of Timur. Besides spreading Sufi-infused Islam,

---

[80]Mirza Waheed, *The Book of Gold Leaves* (New Delhi: Viking, 2014).

he left an enduring legacy by introducing carpet-making, shawl-weaving and the Central Asian style of architecture in Kashmir.

Since women were not allowed into the main prayer hall, Mahum and I sat with others on the cobbled platform outside. There was the occasional murmur of conversation as women caught up with the week's happenings, but, for the most part, we sat in quiet conviviality. In the compound, families took a stroll. A young boy scampered behind his father with a kite, eager to set it aflight and have it glide in wild abandon.

The etymology—with 'khanqah' signifying a meeting hall for Sufis or a guest house for travellers, and 'mualla' a shine—hence, Khanqah-i-Mualla seemed apt. The shrine was indeed, a meeting place for travellers in search of faith.

Later, Mahum and I walked along the terrace that wraps itself around the main building, to reach the main edifice and then, the women's gallery at the back. Inside, an old woman, dressed in a traditional white headscarf, with numerous gold ear hoops, graciously greeted us. Then, turning away, she faced the wall, murmured prayers and was soon immersed in what seemed to be an intensely private communion.

A few days before our visit, Mahum had explained to me the special allure that Kashmir's shrines held for her. 'Where else can you, as a woman just sit? The mountains, the river banks, the overarching trees—all these wonderful spaces—they belong to men. If I feel like stretching out on the grass like so many young boys, I will have to take along my grandmother as a chaperone. Shrines, on the other hand—they give me the space to just be.'

I saw what Mahum meant when, some days later, as I walked past the Khanqah, I saw two women relaxing and feeding pigeons on the cobbled platform.

A few days later, when I visited Jamia Masjid—the grand mosque built by Sikandar Shah in (roughly) 1400 AD, and enlarged by his son so it could accommodate up to 30,000 devotees—my friend Ifra Reshi drew my attention to the special seating arrangements at the back for women (otherwise uncommon in mosques). In the Mughal-styled gardens, I spied a girl reading all alone under a tree. Ifra told me that school girls often lingered in the gardens of the masjid to while away their time before tuition classes. It was an accepted social space.

I recalled a conversation with Mahum in which she had spoken of what shrines meant for the women of her family.

'If my mother was stressed, we would try to go to Chrar-e-Sharief or come to Khanqah. And while a shrine does not welcome women under its central dome, the way it does men, there is a small room at the back where they are allowed to sit and pray. This is unlike masjids, many of which don't have have special rooms for women, the assumption being that women will pray from home. Shrines are radical spaces where women can experience spirituality, chat with a friend or even have something to eat afterwards,' she explained.

Shrines are also the perfect venues for women to organize social events like *zar kasai*, or the first hair-cut of a child, finalize matters related to marriages and distribute *tehar*, the yellow, spicy rice on festive occasions. These social spaces also let women stay on to talk to one another or buy halwa or nadur-monji (fried lotus roots) from shops close by.

R, whose house I lived in as a paying-guest, told me she loved going to the Hazratbal Shrine. At home she was lonely, often bullied by her sister- or mother-in-law and was always worried about her husband's struggles with unemployment. But at the shrine, she found solace in spirituality and the joys of of 'suhbah' (a term loosely signifying gatherings that offer companionship).

◆

What makes shrines more accommodating spaces for women as compared to the predominantly male-dominated mosques? Is it because shrines are rooted in Sufi mysticism which, by its very nature, puts emphasis on private and personal experiences, rather than literary and institutional certification? What makes shrines so beloved is their accessibility. Tombs or shrines were built to honour saints—men and women— recognized as *walis* or friends of God who can intercede on behalf of the faithful. Devotees and troubled souls believe the saint is still alive and one can ask for a boon by tying a ribbon which will be untied when granted. A token sum of money is offered for the shrine's maintenance. Since prayers to *walis* and the associated rituals do not require special knowledge of religious texts, ordinary women feel empowered—confident that they are on equal terms with learned men of books while pleading with saints.

This ease of access and negotiation was evident when Mahum and I visited Dastgeer Sahib, the Sufi shrine built in memory of Sheikh Abdul Qadir Gilani (also known as 'Gous-e-Azam' and 'Dastgeer Sahib'), founder of the Sufi order that came to be known as the Qadri Silsila.[81] Many women spoke of how the 'pir' would never fail to come to their aid if invoked in

---

[81]While the Persian Gous-e-Azam never even visited the Valley, 'some of his descendants, almost a score of generations removed are believed to have settled in Kashmir and established this shrine in his memory'. See Sohail Hashmi, 'Speaking of Synthesis', *Kafila*, in <https://kafila.org/2011/07/01/speaking-of-synthesis-kashmir-heritage-architecture-shrines/>, 1 July 2011, accessed on 14 July 2016.

times of adversary. 'Ya Dastgeer,' I heard them exclaim, much like the boatmen paddling through Srinagar's waterways, who called out to him in stormy weather. A woman from south Kashmir spoke of her gratitude because the heavy rains in the spring of 2015 had stopped and the fears of another flood had abated.

If shrines hold a key place in several women's lives in Kashmir, it is also because of the sway of the Kashmiri woman mystic, Lal Ded. The travails of being married at an early age, and the oppression she suffered at the hands of her mother-in-law strike a deep chord of empathy among women here, as does her journey towards liberty by becoming a wandering preacher, singing verses or vaks, and preaching love and faith.

In a shrine, a woman can kneel, arms outstretched and urge the saint to pay heed to the secrets of her heart. 'Where else can I go?' she will beseech; or wail aloud expressing her deepest anguish; or kiss the floor. Rubaina, a young woman told me that she visited shrines when she felt like crying her heart out.

Journalist Aliya Bashir has created small vignettes of the various women thronging the various Sufi shrines of Kashmir[82]—a family brings a listless, dispirited daughter to sing hymns and participate in an Urs;[83] a woman from Budgam, whose son had suffered an enforced disappearance, weeps and seeks solace and a young girl fervently appeals to the saint at Makhdoom Sahib to grant her the grades she

---

[82]The land of Kashmir Sufi saints, women find devotion and healing. Women's News Network:
http://www.womennewsnetwork.net/2013/06/25/kashmir-sufi-saints-women/
[83]An Urs is the death anniversary of a saint. But the term also signifies a wedding and is a metaphor for the union of the saint's soul with God.

needs to become a doctor.

Such vignettes reinforce what Dr Arshad Hussain of the mental health hospital in Rainawari said about shrines being spaces of great healing. He told me that shrines formed the strongest psychotherapeutic chambers in Kashmir particularly in conflict. There was a time, he explained, when there was such a strong trust deficit you could not confide in your close relatives or neighbours. Shrines, were receptacles of secrets, fears and angst. They were places for abreaction especially for women of lower middle class. The shrines, he explained, not only enabled them to abreact emotionally but seemed to offer something else—an answer linked to faith—a spiritual anchor that was very important.

◆

The intersection of religion and politics was very evident when I had visited the Jamia Masjid. This was, I was told, the Mirwaiz (head preacher) stronghold as was evident from the numerous photographs of his that hung from stalls in the adjoining market. The title Mirwaiz has been in use since 1901 and, according to historian Sir Walter Lawrence, Kashmir's Muslims were increasingly divided along loyalties owed to two Mirwaizes—the Mirwaiz of the Jamia and the Mirwaiz of the Khanqah which was more broadly representative of the Sufi path.[84]

In the 1930s, Mirwaiz Yusuf Shah of Jamia introduced a young Sheikh Abdullah from the pulpit. The two had joined hands to oppose Maharaja Hari Singh and had gone on to form the All Jammu and Kashmir Muslim Conference(AJKMC).

Historian Mridu Rai in her book notes how in the limited

---

[84]Walter Lawrence, *The Valley of Kashmir* (London: H. Frowde, 1895).

space for discourse under Dogra rule, the AJKMC was able to bring a 'movement that consistently displayed an acute religious sensibility, even as it alluded to a wider regional identity bridging the communitarian divide.'[85]

The Mirwaiz and Sheikh Abdullah parted ways in 1939 when the AJKC was dissolved and the National Conference was formed. An intense rivalry between the two sprang up. Supporters of the Sheikh were called called 'shers' or 'lions' (alluding to the Sheikh's moniker, 'Lion of Kashmir'), and the Mirwaiz's followers being referred to as 'bakras' or 'goats' (alluding to the clergy's beard). A peace treaty was later brokered. Today, descendants of both figures continue to play their respective roles in the state's complex political scenario.

---

[85]*Hindu Rulers, Muslim Subjects: Islam, Rights and History of Kashmir*, by Mridu Rai

Chapter Nine

CONCERN OR CONTROL?
The Complexities of Occupation

Shortly after our visit to the shrines, Mahum and I met for lunch at a Ladakhi café where, over noodles, we discussed the patriarchal nature of both occupation and society and notions of 'care', 'control' and 'concern'. Using apt terminology, Mahum made a powerful observation, 'Control and care seem to work, side by side, much like the way the army deploys its counter-insurgency measures *and* the Sadbhavana programme.[86] In a hegemonic setup, cruelty and compassion ride together and can be so effectively applied that it doesn't get recognized as oppression.'

---

[86]'[The] Army has undertaken a large number of Military Civic Action programmes aimed at "Wining the Hearts and Minds" of the people in J&K and North Eastern States, as part of a strategy for conflict resolution. These programmes aim to achieve the following:
  (a) Fulfilling the needs of the peoples and to alleviate their problems.
  (b) Development of remote and inaccessible areas where civil administration is barely existent.
  (c) Assuaging the feeling of alienation and moulding public opinion towards peace and development.'
See 'Operation Sadbhavana', *Ministry of Information & Broadcasting*, in <http://inbministry.blogspot.in/2013/03/operation-sadbhavana.html>, accessed on 18 July 2016.

Her remarks spurred me on to explore the nature of occupation in the borderlands of north Kashmir where thousands of troops have a pincer-like grip on the towns and villages.

A gleaning of new understanding on the concerns of these populations came with the national elections of 2014. I had earlier subscribed to the popular perception that the voter turnout in the Valley was an indicator of the average Kashmiri's belief in India's democratic principles until successive visits toppled such assumptions.

So, when the Hurriyat called for a boycott of the national elections in 2014 with Chairman Syed Ali Geelani denouncing mainstream political parties as 'collaborators'[87], I could understand why several districts in south Kashmir paid heed. They made a strong statement of resistance—with Tral, the bastion of a new generation of militants, registering a voter turnout of only 1.3 per cent and Pulwama, 6.3 per cent.[88] What puzzled me was the high voter turnout in the more militarized zones of north Kashmir. What did that convey?

Some political observers urged me to take a nuanced look and understand why militarization *compels* people to engage with the political system? Why did people in highly militarized zones feel the need for a local MLA or a political

---

[87]Shuja-Ul-Haq, 'Hurriyat's Syed Ali Geelani Calls for Boycott of 2014 Polls', *India Today*, 2 November 2013.

[88]Sanjay Kak, 'Ballot Bullet Stone', *Caravan*, September 2014. Kak states: 'In the decrepit Electric Revenue office nearby, Tral 57 D was not doing [well]: one vote that morning out of a possible 1,108. One vote at Tral 51 A, in the Government Girls Higher Secondary School—and that from a former member of the legislative assembly. The polling agents were missing here, too. But since the Election Commission had equipped booths with webcams and high-speed internet dongles, perhaps somewhere far away and safe, someone had kept tabs on the two voters who had shown up so far at Tral 53 C, the one voter at Tral 54 A (a former minister), and the zero voters at Tral 55 B.'

leader? Was it for *bijli-paani-sadak?* Or is it something much more crucial?

I learnt people in militarized zones voted simply to secure themselves. They voted because they must have a local political interface with the security forces for times such as when they need to get information about a relative in detention. They voted to get a form of identification. And sometimes, it was to chart a safe passage for themselves and their families in a land of all-pervasive surveillance.

◆

This surveillance and control by the military is not restricted to just merely the visual—evident in the omnipresence of checkposts, or the massive gated barriers in towns like Boniyar or the huge bunkers that rear up in the chowks. It is manifested in the way the military controls the economy, means of livelihood and social spaces since there is very little civil aid and civic infrastructure.

Most of the funds of Operation Sadbhavana are spent here and the army through its civic action programmes exercises its grip over basic amenities like water supply and electrification. It provides a means of livelihood through animal husbandry or career opportunities by teaming up with corporates and state tourism board.

The army provides education through its highly subsidized Goodwill Schools[89] and also provides local employment for teachers. It is the army that runs computer-literacy classes. And, it is the army that controls everyday matters—from

---

[89]'Indian Army over the years has established 46 Army Goodwill Schools and rendered assistance to approximately 11 schools in remote areas. See *Army Goodwill Schools*, in <http://www.armygoodwillschool.in/>, accessed on 18 July 2016.

whether cricket tournaments can be held to how traffic is to move.

It is this complexity of occupation that Mohamad Junaid refers to in his insightful essay pointing out how the occupying state is seen as providing means of livelihood even as it destroys existing ones or is seen as providing security even while being the source of insecurity.[90]

◆

Another strategic arm of governance is through operations of the National Hydropower Corporation (NHPC) with its numerous dams and power plants that many Kashmiris view with suspicion. Anthropologist and researcher Mona Bhan, in an illuminating essay, notes:

> For many Kashmiris, the construction of at least twelve dams in the J&K state to harness its water resources is as indubitable an expression of India's illegitimate rule in the region as its extensive military hold over Kashmir. With roughly 131,840 acres of land in J&K under the Indian military and thousands of acres under the control of the National Hydropower Corporation— India's premier agency for hydropower development— Kashmiris view the NHPC as the corporate arm of India's occupation.[91]

---

[90]Mohamad Junaid, 'Life and Death under Occupation', *Everyday Occupations: Experiencing Militarism in South Asia and the Middle East,* edited by Kamala Visweswaran (Pennsylvania: University of Pennsylvania Press, 2013), p. 177.
[91]Mona Bhan, 'Morality and Martyrdom: Dams, Dharma, and the Cultural Politics of Work in Indian-occupied Kashmir', *Academia.edu,* in <http://www.academia.edu/9138810/Morality_and_Martyrdom_Dams_Dharma_and_the_Cultural_Politics_of_Work_in_Indian-occupied_Kashmir>, accessed on 18 July 2016.

In the wake of several protests against NHPC and questions in the Legislative Assembly, the company now states that it employs 'humanitarian discourse', observes Bhan, to prove that its corporate action is motivated by 'care, compassion and responsibility, rather than merely an obsessive drive for profit or control, motivate corporate action'. Dam building, it is suggested, is moral work, and will help 'heal mental and psychological wounds from over two decades of conflict' by boosting the self-esteem of an alienated population and offering them employment.

Bhan observes, however, that such 'meanings of corporate magnanimity are vigorously debated and challenged'.[92]

It was with these complexities of occupation in mind that I wanted to travel and interact with Razia Sultan of Boniyar, Uri, in September 2014.

◆

I had been told Razia was a remarkable woman, who had been incarcerated for many years in jail, because she asked too many questions and went on a relentless search for her missing father; that she had played a vital role in helping to document the presence of mass anonymous graves in north Kashmir and that she was clearly a leader of sorts in her town. But, there were also suspicions raised—that she was close to the army and the state and worked in association with their projects. I was intrigued by this seeming contradiction. We met very briefly in Srinagar on a September afternoon. Rain was coming down hard and she left hastily to catch her shared Sumo. Like many plans, my proposed visit to her town was washed away.

---

[92]Ibid.

About a fortnight after cellular networks came crawling back to life, I received a call from Razia who told me the situation in Uri had been alarming, the river had changed course, and there was widespread damage. By then, I had returned to Mumbai, and could only offer words of commiseration.

We remained sporadically in touch and finally met in Srinagar almost a year after our first hurried encounter. Talking at leisure, Razia began her story with the day her father failed to return home.

On 13 May 1990, Raja Ali Mardan left his home in Bala, Boniyar, after breakfast. He said goodbye to his fourteen-year-old daughter, Razia—one of two sisters and a brother—and set off for his cooperative office carrying with him a sum of rupees 1 lakh in cash.

Later that evening, when Razia and her younger sister, who was not keeping well, visited a peer (mendicant) to procure a 'taaveez' (talisman), a commotion broke out. The mendicant's son, who had been picked up for inquiries, had been brought back, and army officials started questioning those waiting in the house. Razia recalled, 'A major asked me who I was and seemed taken aback when I added my father's name to my own. He abruptly told my sister and me that our father would not come home that night and warned us not to go home, saying we would get killed. We were very upset, but decided to stay put for the night.'

Once home, their mother confirmed that their father had not returned that night. Bystanders had seen him being picked up and taken away in a car near Boniyar market, down a road lined with army camps and bunkers. It was claimed that he had been trying, in vain, to jump out.

Razia's mother, her children in tow, tried filing a missing

person's complaint with the SHO, but the police refused to register an FIR—this, despite the fact that Razia revealed her conversation with the major of the 3rd Sikh Regiment and her belief that he was aware of, if not involved with, the alleged abduction. In the absence of active police action, Razia and her mother were compelled to begin a search of their own in jails, police stations, interrogation centres, militant hideouts, even across the border, graveyards, and whenever there was the discovery of a dead body or human remains.[93]

Razia's refusal to stop the search became awkward for the security agencies and there were many raids at her home. Militants, too, were suspicious because of her constant visits to security camps. In 1995, Razia was summoned to Baramulla where she complained of the raids. In reprisal, a poster claiming she was wanted for being part of the militancy was put up and she was forced to flee to Srinagar. Married at a very young age, Razia was also forced to look after a small child single-handedly because her husband abandoned her, unable to take the pressure of her circumstances.

She was also not able to shake off the security forces and was picked up by the Rashtriya Rifles when she came back to Baramulla to attend a wedding. Handed over to the Joint Interrogation Centre, Razia was booked under the draconian PSA and Terrorism and Disruptive Activities (Prevention) Act (TADA) for allegedly being involved with unlawful activities. This was the beginning of the phase of serial detentions—

---

[93]Razia's investigations acted as valuable signposts when a documentation of mass anonymous graves began soon after 2005. Her work has been openly acknowledged by the SHRC's report of 2011. She is amongst those who chose not to stay anonymous. See *The SHRC on Unmarked Graces: The Investigation Report*, in <http://www.kashmirlife.net/full-text-of-the-enquiry-report-of-the-investigation-team-of-jak-shrc-on-unmarked-graves-in-north-kashmir-1702/>, 26 August 2011, accessed on 18 July 2016.

long spells in jail—first for thirteen months and then for another twenty-four. In 2003, she was picked up yet again by the Special Task Force (STF) and was sent to the infamous interrogation centre in Srinagar known as Cargo. She claimed that during her incarcerations she was severely tortured. She received a long gash across the head and, holding up her hand, she showed me the scar across her wrist.

'*Army neh, police neh, STF neh jeena hi haram kar diya tha,*' ('The army, the police and the STF made life impossible')[94] she declared. Why, I asked her, did the security agencies continue to hound and persecute her. She said that perhaps it was because she refused to stop her search. Or was it because she, a woman, would not conform to being a meek and submissive victim? Or because she resisted turning into an informer despite pressure by the forces? Ironically, militant groups too were suspicious of her activities.

It was only after political intervention by a senior Congress leader, who demanded that the charges against Razia be substantiated or that she be left alone, that the security forces backed down.

The years of extensive search for her father and the methodical way she processed information made her a very valuable researcher when documentation on the mass anonymous graves of north Kashmir began. She said, she was once alerted to the presence of grisly human remains and a skull by the loud chattering of monkeys near a graveyard. Despite threats by Ikhwanis she agreed to give witness to the probe conducted into mass graves by Senior Superintendent,

---

[94]Razia's trials have been recorded in 'Voices Unheard', *Jammu Kashmir Coalition of Civil Society*, Volume 7, in <http://www.jkccs.net/wp-content/uploads/2015/02/Voices-Unherad-vol-7.doc>, accessed on 18 July 2016.

Bashir Itoo, for the SHRC and chose not to remain anonymous. She is a prominent figure in the town and takes up causes ranging from pension schemes to livelihood options for widows as well as the younger generation. She, herself, is a contractor for undertaking works under the Mahatma Gandhi National Rural Emplopyment Guarantee Act and often drives a JCB herself.

Does the nature of this work leave her open to mistrust and suspicion by some civilians?

In a controlled economy, where contracts are granted by the military, either directly or indirectly—and in a highly fractured society where terms like 'informers' and 'collaborators' are loosely flung—has Razia, perhaps, been seen as having compromised herself? Is that why she remains a figure of mystery?

A prominent human rights lawyer told me that he was convinced that the innuendoes and slurs against Razia were just character assassination. They arose, he said, because she was a woman operating in an increasingly hostile and complex zone. Resentment was inevitable, he said and added that activists in cities and towns have spaces she does not enjoy.

Interestingly, Razia's work as a contractor saw her opposing the NHPC. While the initial bone of contention was the non-payment of dues, later, her concerns became more far-ranging—with the NHPC being viewed as an encroacher, trying to control Kashmir's resources. Given how passionately Razia spoke about the destruction of land and the havoc caused to grazing grounds, I was not surprised when she told me that there had been some talk of fielding her as a candidate should she wish to join mainstream politics.

After our lengthy conversation, we made plans to leave for Uri the next day. She did not show up at the place we had agreed to meet. Her phone remained switched off. I had been told she was unpredictable but the warmth she had shown to me the previous day had disarmed me.

Did Razia worry that my presence as a stranger would raise questions? Was she unsure about my motives? Or was I reading too much into her disappearance—was she simply reclusive?

Even as I circled these questions, I recalled author Nadine Gordimer's observation: 'Nothing is simple in a life and a country where conflict breaks up all consistency of character.'[95]

---

[95]Nadine Gordimer, *My Son's Story* (London: Bloomsbury, 1990), p. 193.

Chapter Ten

I CAN SAVE MYSELF

Dissent and Feminism in a New Millenium

It was with an amazing sense of déjà vu that I scrolled down Facebook on an August afternoon, six years after 2010. Once again, there were images of another Kashmir uprising, this time sparked by Burhan Wani's killing. I gazed at the scene of women on the streets with full-throated cries of azadi at Baramulla. Underneath was the caption: 'Misguided', 'jihadi', 'illiterate' 'oppressed' women of Kashmir voicing their opinions in huge numbers. Indian feminists have been telling us that we need azadi not from India but from patriarchy. Are you watching this IndFem?'

The comment was by the feisty Essar Batool, whose Twitter handle, 'a girl with opinions', typifies the new age woman of Kashmir. She and other like-minded young women like Mahum, Natasha Rather, Farhana Latief, Inshah Malik and many many others fight against patriarchal norms in society but are also outspoken about the brutal nature of the occupation and will have no truck with 'nationalist' feminism which wants to delink gender from the larger questions of Kashmir's future.

This entanglement of gender with religion and other identities such as political that Kashmiri women engage with has been articulated by researcher/activist Dr Inshah Malik in her paper in which she looks at how women are in a relationship with Islam in diverse ways:

> There are women with a Muslim community identity, who may or may not be practising Muslims when they intervene in political action. Yet, though their sources of resistance are multiple, they are almost invariably cast in religious/cultural terms, forgetting that in all these cases, women are both challenging the Indian state/occupation as well as the patriarchy of militarism alongside that of the community. Hence, like women elsewhere, they have continually been refashioning gender identity within the community and within the politics of resistance, but in more culturally appropriate ways.[96]

For many young women like Essar, it was the 2008 uprising that brought about the heightened political consciousness. She told me how her 'zenana' (women's) college actually held a student protest. The immediate provocation had been the Amarnath land row. But the events that followed—the economic blockade which impeded the supply of essential commodities within the Valley,[97] and the violence unleashed on civilians as they attempted to open an alternative route from Muzaffarabad in Pakistan-administered Kashmir to get

---

[96]Inshah Malik, *The Muslim Woman's Struggle for Justice*, in <http://www.india-seminar.com/2013/643/643_inshah_malik.htm>, accessed on 18 July 2016.
[97]See Muzaffar Raina, 'Jammu Begins to Choke Kashmir,' *The Telegraph*, 7 August 2008.

vital supplies[98]—led to more strident protests.

'Earlier, we had shied away from demonstrations. But what we witnessed and the false claims made across mainstream media outlets, upset us deeply. A brigadier on national television argued that the security forces only aimed for the legs of protesters fighting the blockade. Are we to believe these boys were two-years-olds that the bullets aimed at legs hit their chests?

'Enraged, we approached our college principal who, interestingly enough, agreed to support us. She said we were free to protest within the premises but asked us not to raise anti-India slogans.' Soon after, placards screaming, 'Stop killing our boys' were hoisted in the air.

'We marched around the main building,' Essar added. 'At that stage, I was too shy to holler slogans, but I did join the rally. We shared a common wall with SP College and the boys, too, chose to participate—girls would yell a catchphrase and guys would echo the refrain. For once, there was an exchange that had nothing to do with love!'

On the first day, protests lasted for half an hour, but later, a few students, suitably emboldened, marched to the streets to make their anger known. Essar recalled, 'I heard men remark, "*Ab toh azadi aa hi jayegi, ladkiyaan nikli hain bahar!*" ('Now azadi will definitely be ours, the women have come out!')'

For Essar, 2008 was the year when the protective bubble-wrap around her life came off. 'A lot of girls from my generation—from typical middle-class families—went to missionary schools, and led a cocooned existence. Our families had been through a lot in the 1990s—I later learnt that my

---

[98]See Shujaat Bukhari, 'Muzaffarabad Marchers Fired Upon, Five Killed', *The Hindu*, 12 August 2008.

father had, at one point, been detained by security troops—but these events were never spoken about. 2008 changed that.'

Some whiffs of protests found their way even to the missionary schools where politics was never discussed. Fatimah, researcher and writer recounted an amusing anecdote from her days as a student in one such school.

After school had reopened, following the prolonged curfews, the games teacher, one day, ordered the students to sprint across the school ground, in the heat of the afternoon sun. A spark of rebellion must have asserted itself, because, led by Fatimah, who was the school captain, the girls began running around the field shouting the landmark pro-freedom slogan: 'Hum kya chahte: Azadi! Azadi!' Fatimah remembered, 'The school principal was less than pleased. I was told that I came from a respectable family and couldn't do such things!'

◆

'Yeh mat karo, aisa mat karo (Don't do this, don't do that). All these restrictions that society imposes on us to make us submissive' complained Rubaina (name changed), a psychology student, who elaborated on societal strictures as we sat talking on the bund close to the River Jhelum. Rubaina explained how her growing consciousness on how patriarchy functions also intertwined with her political awareness.

She said that from an early age, she had taken on the responsibility of caring for her family and running errands since her mother was ailing and her father had met with an accident. 'I became independent. I learnt how to drive, so I could go to the shops. I even went to the kondur (traditional bakery) that was considered to be a male domain.'

But when her parents recovered, Rubaina started facing restrictions. 'Suddenly it was not okay to do the very things I had been doing all along when they needed my help. I began to critically understand the way patriarchal norms played out in society.' She also realized how conflict hardened the repression. The men's frustration over the oppression by security troops and the anger/helplessness they felt was vented on the women of the family over whom they tried to exercise control.

There were more rigid impositions of a dress code and accepted forms of behaviour. Rubaina told me, 'We are reminded all the time that a "good" girl is docile, wears a headscarf, doesn't talk to men, and seeks the counsel of her parents on all matters—from leaving home, to getting married. A "bad" girl, on the other hand, takes her own decisions—be it in her choice of dress or whom she chooses to talk with.'

She asserted, 'I've been a good girl all these years. But now I would like to be a bad girl. If being good means that I accept the dominance of men in our society—of, say, a father or a brother, then I refuse. I want to make my own choices.'

Rubaina also spoke of how this freedom of free expression was linked to the political. 'In an oppressed territory where survival is difficult, free expressions of emotions are not seen as important. My mother doesn't want to talk about things because she doesn't get a good feeling about it.'

She added, 'The fact is that an occupation also deeply impacts our thought processes. We think we are free but are we? We are under surveillance all the time even on Facebook. All we want to do is escape in consumerist spending at a shopping centre or in buying a new car.'

So, whilst she dreams of an azadi she wants it in synergy with emancipation for women—a freedom that will enable women to take on the responsibility of their own lives.

◆

Rubaina's remarks led me to try and explore a growing trend in gender sensitivity in Kashmir that refuses to restrict conversations on women to just those that are conflict related but encompasses issues like societal restrictions, domestic violence, sexuality and so on.

Says Essar, 'There used to be the feeling that we women should not talk about patriarchy in our society, that it is an internal issue. But we do need to question it and are doing so.'

In the workshops she has conducted, Essar has tackled the need to fight the accepted language of patriarchy whether it is the hierarchical seating during a 'majlis' (gathering)—where women figure last in the pecking-order; or the fact that the most succulent and largest pieces of mutton are reserved only for the male members of the family. (Kashmiris convey the value of a person by the amount and quality of meat they offer).

She also tries to make girls more sexually aware of their bodies. 'If you ask women to draw a uterus, the images they present are hilarious. They have never really given much thought to their bodies. A baby boy's genitals are spoken of with charming epithets—there is even joking amongst themselves about it—but a baby girl is quickly swaddled and hidden. From the very beginning, women are taught to carry a sense of body shame.'

Nadiyah Shafi, a social worker and now a community correspondent with Video Volunteers[99] has attempted, through her work, to bring issues of sexuality out in the open. These

---

[99]Video Volunteers is an organization that believes in empowering marginalized communities by providing video journalism skills so that the community can tell its own stories.

include the challenges that members of the third gender face.[100] Her interview with Zeenat, a third gender person, who spoke of being forced to leave home, met with strong reactions. Zeenat was sacked from her job with a non-governmental organization (NGO) for her open admission of belonging to the third gender group and for pleading for her right to lead a life of dignity. Nadiyah and other members of VV supported her financially and emotionally for many months till she was placed elsewhere.

Nadiyah also conducts gender sensitivity classes in rural districts where subjects like dress code, domestic violence, divorce even the right of a woman to own a mobile and so on have been keenly discussed.

Sajjad Rasool, the state consultant for VV, confessed that in the fight for political rights, certain social issues had been overlooked. And that one of these was violence against women who are 'treated as second class citizens in some of the more rigid sub societies.' VV has adopted a policy of having an equal number of men and women as community reporters and one of them is Aafroze, of Ganderbal district, who wears an abaya and has taken the lead in reporting on domestic violence. She also has some fine accounts of environmental degradation of wetlands to her credit.

◆

When I walked past the Press Colony in Srinagar on April 20 2016, I could not help but notice the heavy presence of

---

[100]For link to Nadiyahs video: http://kashmirunheard.org/2015/08/02/justice-not-given-to-the-third-gender-video-volunteer-nadiya-shafi-reports-from-srinagar/

police personnel and the gaze of curious passersby. Who were these protesters? These young women, placards in hand, were standing in a semicircle denouncing the police and the army for the illegal detention of a minor girl at Handwara following her allegation of molestation by a soldier near a public toilet.

This demonstration was again significant for the way Kashmir's new-age women were taking on patriarchy and oppression in *all* its forms. They were actively supporting this minor girl who had been whisked away immediately after the incident, kept in illegal police confinement and coerced into a video recording (in flagrant violation of laws and norms) absolving the army. The video, which was released on social media platforms and aired by national television networks (in blatant violation of guidelines and laws on coverage of sexual violence) cleverly exploited faultlines in society and a section of the public began casting aspersions on this girl. From being seen as victim, she was now being labelled as an army informer, a girl with loose morals and so on.[101]

Whilst the JKCCS provided legal counsel and fought for her right to be freed from illegal police detention, some young women set up a support group and denounced the manipulation by the state to control narratives. One amongst them, Natasha Rather, spoke out vociferously on how irrelevant questions were being raised by the public, such as why did the girl use a public toilet and who was she speaking with on her mobile. 'Are they suggesting that if she talks to boys or uses a phone she is not worth fighting for?' Natasha demanded.

Mahum, another vocal member of the support group, pointed out how the state effectively prevents discussions

---

[101]http://theladiesfinger.com/handwara/

on gender justice. Similar tactics, she said, had been deployed in the Shopian case with aspersions cast on the morals of Nelofar and Asiya.

She pointed out how the firing on protesters in Handwara and militarization effectively blocked discussions around gender justice. 'How do we have nuanced discussions about issues like gender or anything else when the stress and pressure of living in militarized conditions means that the overwhelming concern now is about lives that have been lost?'

More evidence of the way Kashmir's young women fight complex issues of gender justice and politics came when, later in the year, a magazine claimed that young women were being lured into sex and spy rings by intelligence agencies and editorialized how imams, civil society and elders must monitor the morals and use of mobiles of young girls[102].

Farhana Latief who has a masters degree in law from the Tata Institute of Social Sciences debunked the very premises of the editorial that saw women as 'property'—something that needs guarding. She was also incensed at the way women were seen as 'carriers of morality' who must be kept in check if the fabric of society is to be kept intact. She felt such attempts at control were coming from the growing realisation that women were daring to act 'without the consent of their Lords, their owners, their men.'

♦

This challenging male diktats on morality is extended to conversations around religion. In a lengthy conversation, Essar remarked, how men simply assume they are the *thekedars* of what is right or wrong and she was convinced that one's

---

[102]http://www.kashmirnarrator.com/5645-2/

understanding of Islam cannot come only from bearded men in pulpits.

She added, 'I had begun disliking religion but then realized it was because of the way it was being interpreted by some men. My father gifted me the book *Rights of Women in Islam* by Ayatollah Murtaza Muttaharri that changed my understanding of religion completely.

She realized there was a difference between what Islam, as a religion, said about women and the cultural context within which Islam was practised. 'So, while Islam says women have property rights, Kashmiri society considers a woman *laalchi*, (greedy) if she protests when her property is usurped.

'Similarly, Islam grants a woman the right to choose a man—even ask for him—for a marriage contract. But our cultural milieu is such that, far from being encouraged to exercise this right, a woman is made to go along with her parents' wishes, to please them and protect the family's izzat when it comes to exercising a choice over whom one is to marry!'

One of the most animated and emotive conversations taking place, not just in Kashmir but throughout the world, revolves around Islam's injunctions to dress modestly, manifested for women through the hijab (head scarf) and the various attires used to cover the body (abaya/burqa/ and so on). This spurs the question: Is wearing the hijab/ abaya then a demonstration of religious obligation? Or does it flow from societal imposition? Or then, is it an assertion of an identity—an act of free will?

The varied and nuanced responses by women in Kashmir on why they choose or then did not choose the hijab/abaya was a fascinating exploration of what female freedom really means.

I learnt that in the nineties there were militant organizations like the Allah Tigers and radical fora like Asiya Andrabi's Dukhtaran-e-Millat that used coercive tactics to force women to cover up and wear burqa but these groups did not gain much traction in society. They stopped their coercive tactics. But as young Asma, a teacher in Shopian who wears the hijab, and Uzma Qureishi who wears a burqa told me, many women are now *choosing* this attire as an affirmation of their faith and that it was an informed decision. Uzma made an interesting observation of how she differed in opinion from men who claimed wearing hijab or burqa could afford some degree of protection.

'I have argued with men of how elderly women and even babies have been targets of sexual violence. A burqa doesn't necessarily spell safety. One wears it for a different reason.'

A young student in Shopian told me she was proud of sporting the hijab as a way of proclaiming a definite Kashmiri Muslim identity, and as a badge of resistance.

Dress code becomes even more complex when western sensitivity is used to project the wearing of abaya as regressive and another form of imposition is sought. This inverse imposition became evident in 2016 when a private school sacked a teacher who insisted on wearing the abaya. A former pupil defended the school's action saying a school had to be seen as progressive and liberal.

Farhana, participating in a social media debate, countered this by saying that the choice of dress is a personal one and is highly influenced by the culture of a place and, in the context of Kashmir, by its religious practices. By not allowing her to wear the abaya wasn't the state guilty of interfering in her religious rights? She also explained that many women found it easier in their families to be able to work outside the home if they wore the abaya and valued this economic independence. 'We need to respect these choices,' she added.

Farhana, who chooses to wear the hijab, says it became part of her understanding of identity politics when she travelled extensively in India. 'People from various sides of the political spectrum—far right and left—were making all kinds of assumptions of me being oppressed.'

Essar says the notion that one has become radicalized because one chooses to wear a certain kind of attire is naïve. 'You just can't assume that a Muslim woman who wears the hijab is being subjected to patriarchial rules or is dumb. Just because I cover my head doesn't mean that I am covering my brains as well, or that I am submissive. Maybe, I just want to break the stereotypes perpetuated by Islamophobes and people from the western world,' she added.

She is equally scathing about Muslim men who choose to impose their notions of modesty on women. 'Islam has standards of modesty for women *and* men. But men sexualize a woman's body just to maintain their hegemony. Here, let us also talk about the obnoxious way in which some of the men dress. They believe that they can wear low-waisted jeans that reveal their butts, or scratch their balls in public, and people like me will not get offended?'

The assertion of a strong statement by choosing or then not wearing the hijab is evident when someone like Rubaina told me that she has abandoned the headscarf because she sees it as being submissive in society. 'I'm not a good girl any more,' she told me.

And both Munawara and Zamruda questioned me when I wrapped a duppatta around my head wanting to know if it had been at the behest of a man.

That women in Kashmir are increasingly making choices

became evident in this humorous post on Facebook by a young woman:

'Some want to put the hijab on me and save me. Some want to take the hijab off me and save me. Just give me a break, man! I can save myself.'

EPILOGUE

My shoes and socks were soaked. As I waded through ankle-deep water to get to my log hut at the edge of Nigeen Lake, I ran over my schedule for the next week and decided to visit Lal Ded, Srinagar's largest maternity hospital.

Little did I know that a river would run through the hospital and most of Srinagar and almost half a year would pass before I would be able to keep the appointment.

For the next four days it rained incessantly. From my room that lay snuggled under the branches of a towering chinar, I gazed at the lake. Birds scuttled for shelter, and pond herons brushed past my window, trying, in vain, to seek shelter. Hari Parbat, across the lake, remained swathed in clouds. It was wild. It was wonderful.

And then it wasn't. My landlord warned me that I would be asked to shift out if the water levels of the lake rose. On 7 September 2014, as water crept across the walkway near my door, I called my friend Sameena in Rajbagh, who had earlier offered me her home. Hurriedly, she informed me that water was roaring past the second floor of her building. My landlord, on his part, began frantically searching for a family that could accommodate me.

Soon, I was wading through the lawn adjoining the lake

with my laptop, a phone and a plastic bag with three sets of clothes. Bashir—who had, just a week ago, at dawn, taken me for a glorious ride in his shikara to a vegetable market—now paddled through the Nigeen waters that continued to rise.

It was a surreal Sunday. The sun was shining, and Srinagar was drowning. Through Facebook, I learnt that the Jhelum had breached its banks, inundating large parts of the city in its angry, swirling waters. At least, I had a roof over my head.

The next day from my quarters, I watched members of the Hanji community that lives by the waters of the lakes, gathering cows and goats, people and belongings—washing machines, mattresses, stoves and gas cylinders—in shikaras, and taking them across the lake.

A day later, the family that had accommodated me, asked me to leave. They feared that the waters would also enter their home. I had little cash and the ATMs had stopped functioning. The cellphone network was dead, and I could contact no one. I traced my way to the Kashmir University and to a relief camp run by volunteers from the academic community. Arzoo, the wife of a professor, invited me for a cup of tea, and then took me into her home, to share whatever she had for as long as the 'sehlab' prevailed.

Over the next few days, her husband, Dr Iqbal, set out every morning to help with rescue and relief operations, while Arzoo and I combed television channels, desperate for news; or joined the groups clustered near mobile towers in a frantic bid to catch flickering network signals.

A week later, I was able to find transport to the airport. I joined the hundreds fleeing Srinagar. I could not bring myself to look out of the window of the aircraft. I could not bear to watch the city that still continued to be submerged in the river waters. I could not bring myself to be a witness to the agony that the people of this land were facing.

◆

In late March 2015, I returned to a guest house by the Nigeen Lake. From my window, I could hear the tonk-tonk-tonk of construction and I could see an artisan chiselling beams for a new house boat. I spotted carpenters sawing and masons repairing and rebuilding. A city was reasserting itself much like the green shoots and branches of spring that sprouted everywhere.

I visited Munawara. She grabbed my hand and took me on a survey of her house and that of her parents. She showed me tell-tale marks high up on the wall of the ground floor of her residence—'the flood waters had reached *here*.' She told me how she had coordinated rescue and relief efforts in her neighbourhood—how ladders were hoisted and the aged were helped to clamber out of windows and across roofs to the upper floor of her dwelling. She spoke of how an infant was placed in a small carry bag and gently ferried across the rooftops. For several days, Munawara's house sheltered some thirty homeless people.

We exchanged notes on how terrified we were when, a week after the floods, a sudden storm blew up and lightning zig-zagged across the sky.

Munawara smiled, 'During the crash of thunder, I told all those who sat huddled in my room that I had spent the best years of my life weeping, I was not going to die like that. I would go laughing. And I burst out laughing. And soon after, the rain stopped. The storm was gone.'

Munawara laughed out uproariously once again.

◆

Next, I visited Sameena in Rajbagh. Lawns, once lush, had transformed into mud-paths, and houses, reduced to rubble, or pulled down, formed an eerie backdrop. Rajbagh was still to recover. Sameena took me to the top of a stairway and pointed to the balustrade from where she had swung her legs over and climbed into a shikara brought by Khanyaar's fifteen-year-old boys. They took her to to Abdullah Bridge where she waited with others who had been displaced. A family took her in and then helped her into one of several flimsy dinghies. The men swam in the dark and dirty waters, gently pushing the dinghies along, until they reached the higher slopes on the edge of the Dal. 'For them, I am grateful,' she said.

◆

During the floods in Srinagar, I had watched news channels relaying terrible stories about the Lal Ded Hospital—about patients being left to their fate, while doctors ran away to safer areas. Six months later, I visited this 700-bedded government-run hospital by the banks of the Jhelum to find out what really happened.

Carefully working my way across stone and debris, I went inside to meet Dr Shehnaz Taing, head of the gynaecology and obstetrics department.

Despite a hectic schedule, she graciously shared time for memories of the crisis of the nineties during the years of militancy. Many doctors and paramedics—largely from the Pandit community—had fled. It took a number of years to replace the workforce especially as exams could not be held. An extremely depleted team of doctors struggled to cope since the peripheral health services had collapsed. Sometimes, there were three to five women sitting on the same bed. There were huge difficulties in getting to the hospital for emergencies during curfews. 'Our ambulances would be stopped and checked. We were made to get down and stand in the street in the middle of the night. It was so frightening!' she said.

The patients suffered acutely. There were many cases of ruptured uterus and other complications because of the delays and late referrals by the peripheries.

But, eventually, the hospital recovered to become Srinagar's largest maternal, gynaecological and obstetrics centre with 634 patients given attention in the OPDs till 1 p.m. and at least 750 till 4 p.m.

On the night of 6 September after a busy day, Dr Taing rushed back to the hospital having received a call that water was entering the premises. She phoned the authorities who assured her that the waters would recede after 3 a.m.

At midnight, the power supply collapsed. The generators were turned on but the oxygen supply had stopped.

Next morning, around 11 a.m., the bund collapsed and water inundated the ground floor of the hospital. The entire staff—sweepers, nurses, attendants, junior residents, doctors, and others—pitched in to cope. Patients were shifted to the upper floors. Deliveries were carried out by candlelight and despite the lack of oxygen, three patients were operated upon.

'One of our consultants, Shylla Mir, knew that her locality was under water. She was desperately worried, but she stayed on. My husband wanted to come and fetch me. But I told him I would not leave.' Dr Taing said.

'When supplies ran out, we asked patients to drink from dextrose bottles. Some of us ate raw rice and sugar. As a member of the staff put it: *'Hum toh Titanic ho gaye.'* ('We are now in the Titanic.')

Army helicopters whizzed overhead ferrying tourists. As in so many parts of Srinagar, it was not the government but the community-based efforts that brought some relief to the marooned hospital. At 3 p.m., two young boys paddled by in a boat and asked what was most urgently required. 'They were our angels,' Dr Taing recalled. 'Two hours later, they brought biscuits and candles. We distributed the biscuits, first among the children, then the patients and attendants.'

By the evening of 8 September, that was a Monday, the hospital had turned into a giant shelter. There was no electricity, no water and no supplies. They worked in the dark, for there were no candles left, and torn duppattas were used to cover wounds. When it seemed like little else that could be offered by way of medical care, doctors, patients and staff, who had spent forty-eight harrowing hours on the premises, began leaving.

The medical superintendent drew up an evacuation plan and a human chain was formed to help the mothers and their infants squeeze through a gap in the wall and walk across the broken bund, past a footbridge and up towards a community camp set up by politician Altaf Bukhari.

◆

Even now, I try to picture those stirring images. There is a long row of women, who have given birth in the midst of destruction, their babies, a new generation, are tied securely to their bodies with a duppatta. I see them as they walk, slowly, cautiously, confidently, across the broken embankment, past seething waters, to the safety of their community and their people.

Once more, they shine.

Acknowledgements

I would like to thank:

All the women who shared their experiences, offered me their trust and gifted me their stories to make of them what I would. Without their magnanimity there would be no book.

Dilnaz Boga, who initiated my Kashmir journey by inviting me to visit in 2010, and who inspired me with her passion and knowledge of the region. There have been many memorable journeys since and hopefully we will be *humsafars* for many more.

Omar Qadri, whose home we barged into during a curfew and who later sparked the idea of granting a gender perspective to the Kashmir struggle; shukriya for Lolab, for kebabs, a strong friendship and many eventful trips.

Arif Ayaz Parrey who, over the phone, invited me—a stranger—to visit his home, and along with Tawheed Dar and Shahid Yousuf Gilkar introduced me to south Kashmir; Arif continues to stimulate and provoke with his unique insights and friendship.

Nasir Patigaru for his assistance in arranging field trips and whose sensitivity to suffering helped me understand resilience.

Habeel Iqbal, Abdul Basit, Bari Maqbool and others whose invaluable help and wonderful hospitality make south

Kashmir yatras almost mandatory.

Fayaz Ahmad Dar and the Mool team—Lubna, Saquib, Umair, Hadiya—for camping trips, hikes and heritage walks in downtown Srinagar and the animated, off-the-beaten-track discussions.

Aala Fazili, Umair Gul, Khalid Fayaz, Nimer Qayoom, Malik Sajad, Salim Malik, Majid Maqbool and Junaid Rather for the dosti and chai in the university canteens, cafes, the bund and Peerzoo; and Nayeem Mohammed, Irfan Mehraj, Junaid Nabi Bazaz and Mir Suhail for their sparkling company, discussions and the Hollywood Café times—all these young people inspire with their unwavering passion for the cause.

Parvaiz Bukhari and Mohamad Junaid whose writings helped light up my understanding of the complexities of occupation.

Moi, MP, Johnnybhai, Aijaz and others who introduced me to the joys of the waterfront and shikara rides on calm days; and for their camaraderie when the waters rose and lightning ripped the sky.

Arzoo and Dr Jahangir Iqbal for giving me not just shelter but the warmth of a home during the floods—acts of supreme generosity of the heart and spirit.

Lawyers, doctors, legal activists, human rights workers and other professionals quoted in the book who lent me their valuable time and patience.

Aunohita Mojumdar and Laxmi Murthy who encouraged my early forays into writing on Kashmir from a feminist perspective in *Himāl*; Neelam Raaj who accommodated many of my earlier reports on Kashmir in *Crest* and the editors of *India Together* who were always supportive.

And finally, Dharini Bhaskar for her painstaking efforts and empathy.

www.ingramcontent.com/pod-product-compliance
Lightning Source LLC
Chambersburg PA
CBHW020001290326
41935CB00007B/259